Language in Scier
and Fanta

C000060514

Also available from Continuum

The Language of Science, M.A.K. Halliday and Jonathan J. Webster

Language in Science Fiction and Fantasy
The Question of Style

Susan Mandala

continuum

Continuum International Publishing Group

The Tower Building	80 Maiden Lane
11 York Road	Suite 704
London SE1 7NX	New York NY 10038

www.continuumbooks.com

First published 2010
Paperback edition first published 2012

British Library Cataloguing-in-Publication Data
A catalogue record for this book is available from the British Library.

ISBN: 978-1-8470-6301-4 (hardcover)
      978-1-4411-4548-2 (paperback)

Library of Congress Cataloging-in-Publication Data
A catalog record for this book is available from the Library of Congress.

Typeset by Newgen Imaging Systems Pvt Ltd, Chennai, India
Printed and bound in Great Britain

For Kevin

Contents

Acknowledgements

I would like to offer my grateful thanks to a number of people who helped this book come into being. Acknowledgements are due first and foremost to my editors at Continuum, Gurdeep Mattu, Nicole Elliott, and Colleen Coalter, for their patience and advice. Gratitude is also extended to Kevin Higgins, Felicity Breet, Mike Pearce, and Louise Reeve for reading and commenting on drafts. Thanks are also due to Gill Saville, Gareth Hughes, Adina Hughes, and the members of the Graphic Novels Reading Group who have shared and nurtured my interest in science fiction and fantasy over the years. And as always, I would like to thank my students, a daily inspiration in this and all my work.

List of Tables

Chapter 1

Science Fiction and Fantasy: Language, Style, and the Critics

This book is about science fiction and fantasy. Its aim is to demonstrate that a literary-linguistic approach to the language of these texts can shed new light on the issue of style in these genres. In a series of literary-stylistic analyses ranging over a variety of texts, I make the case for style in science fiction and fantasy, showing that it is used to remarkable effect in thematically relevant ways to imagine future Englishes, suggest past Englishes, present the extraordinary as real, and construct compelling characters. Specifically, I will be arguing that (1) the role of style in science fiction and fantasy has been largely misunderstood and thus massively underrated; and (2) that a literary-linguistic study of style in these texts suggests an altogether more positive, even essential role for style in these genres. Before the discussion proper can begin, however, there are several issues of definition to settle. For the purposes of this investigation, what is meant by *style* and *literary-linguistic*? How is *science fiction* defined? What falls under the term *fantasy*?

Style, when interpreted according to its widest definition, as Leech and Short (1981/2007) point out, 'refers to the way in which language is used in a given context, by a given person, for a given purpose, and so on' (9). The literary-linguistic study of style narrows this focus somewhat, and considers *style* to be the way language is used in literature for 'artistic function' (Leech and Short 1981/2007: 11). How, for example, is the style of a particular text, its use of language, instrumental in creating character, or establishing atmosphere, or revealing theme? It is this aspect of style, and questions such as these, that are of interest to the literary linguist. In this investigation, it is the language of fiction, in particular the language of science fiction and fantasy, that is explored. While it has become traditional for studies of science fiction to begin with warnings about how difficult it is to define (e.g. see Lefanu 1988; Moody 2000: 179; Roberts 2000/2006: 1; Rose 1981), Amis's (1960/1963) pioneering definition, still 'the broadest, most accurate, and most comprehensive' (Hillegas 1979: 1), is adopted here:

> [S]cience fiction is that class of prose narrative treating of a situation that could not arise in the world we know, but which is hypothesised on the basis of some innovation in science or technology, or pseudo-science or pseudo-technology, whether human or extra-terrestrial in origin. (Amis 1960/1963: 14)

Fantasy as a term is a bit trickier as it can refer to anything from personal daydreaming to literature that is in anyway non-mimetic (as in Hume's 1984 account of the subject). *Fantasy* in this study, however, refers primarily to *heroic fantasy*, which is also called *high fantasy* and includes *sword and sorcery*. Heroic fantasy is a prose narrative set in an invented and often pre-industrial world where 'magic really works' (quote from Carter 1973: 6–7; see also Sullivan 1996: 311; Swinfen 1984: 5; Wolfe 1986: 52; Zanger 1982: 230).

The preliminaries now out of the way, the case for style in science fiction and fantasy can proceed. I am, of course, not the first person to make this case. Le Guin (1973/1993) and Delany (1969) have both noted the importance of style in these genres, Shippey (1982) had a very credible go with Tolkien's fiction, and recent works by Stockwell (2000), Walsh (2003), Ryder (2003) and Hardy (2003) demonstrate how attention to style in works of science fiction and fantasy can inform interpretation. As the review below will show, however, these are largely minority voices in the study of these genres. While critical evaluations of science fiction and fantasy have mostly succeeded in legitimizing these genres the study of style has fossilized.

Science Fiction and Fantasy: The Road to Respectability

Science fiction and fantasy were, once upon a time, largely ignored by the literary world, dismissed as beneath notice (Attebery 2003: 45) and 'all but invisible' (Wolfe 1986: xi). Prior to the 1960s, as Broderick (2003) notes, 'theorized criticism of sf' was 'almost unknown' (61). Writer/critics Aldiss (1986/2001: ii) and Le Guin (1977/1993: 10) tell the same story. Science fiction 'was not studied' (Le Guin); it was 'virtually a secret movement' (Aldiss); 'there were no schools – in any sense' (Le Guin); there was 'almost no body of sf scholarship (Aldiss); 'it was not taught' (Le Guin); there was almost no student body (Aldiss); 'there were no theories, only the opinion of editors' (Le Guin).

As with science fiction, so with fantasy (Attebery 1992: 105; Wolfe 1986), whose corresponding struggle against nearly complete exile from academe is well documented (e.g. see Parker 1956: 60; Schlobin, ed. 1982: ix; Swinfen 1984: 11). Proponents of the literary fantastic, eager to show that their genre of choice was of true value because it interrogated notions of the 'real' and led readers to experience challenging states of doubt (argued most explicitly by Jackson 1981, but see also Brooke-Rose 1981; Horskotte 2004; Todorov 1973), were especially hard on fantasy, deriding it as 'just' a fairy tale, an ultimately conservative form with a 'relatively rigid narrative structure' (Armitt 2005: 7) that 'manipulated the reader' (Horskotte 2004: 34) into a 'passive' (Jackson 1981: 131) acceptance of 'current ideologies' (Horskotte 2004: 37) as determined by the hegemonic order (Horskotte 2004; Jackson 1981). Both Le Guin (1974/1993: 34) and Swinfen (1984: 1) found the academic response to fantasy so extreme in its negativity as to border on the irrational. Swinfen (1984) put it this way:

[S]ome critics and academics condemn the whole genre with a passion which seems to have its roots in emotion rather than objective critical standards; (Swinfen 1984: 1)

and Le Guin (1974/1993) spoke of

a moral disapproval of fantasy, a disapproval so intense, and often so aggressive, that I cannot help but see it as arising, fundamentally, from fear. (Le Guin 1974/1993: 34)

When the 'respectable' literary world did take an interest in science fiction or fantasy, it insisted, as Parker (1956: 601) noted, on reclassifying it. Tallis (1984), for example, accepted *Nineteen Eighty-Four* and *Gulliver's Travels* as great works of literature by arguing that they were more mimetic than fantastic in their 'scrupulously realistic realization' (Tallis 1984: 193).

Those who did venture to study science fiction and fantasy *as* science fiction and fantasy found themselves writing very much against the literary-critical grain. Le Guin (1974/1993: 2003) wrote with annoyance of 'brush-offs from literary snobs'; Russ (1975: 112) spoke of the 'habitual (and unreflecting) condescension' of mainstream critics with respect to science fiction; Hume (1984: 3) complained of the many who thought fantasy was nothing more than a 'subliterature in lurid covers'; Timmerman (1983: 42) found himself dismayed by all those who assumed fantasy was 'deceptive, illusory and therefore false'; Scholes (1975: 47–8) despaired of those who turned their noses up at science fiction and fantasy without knowing anything about them; Carter (1973: 145) bemoaned those in the literary establishment who continually 'sneered' at sword and sorcery, and who thought that fantasy in general was just cheap entertainment uninterested in the human condition (Carter 1973: 4). Amis (1960/1963), with characteristic wit, summed up the typical establishment response to science fiction like this:

> [H]ostile critics from outside the field will make public utterances upon it revealing a degree of ignorance that would never be tolerated if the subject were Indonesian pottery or Icelandic loan-words in Bantu. (Amis 1960/1963: 129)

For science fiction and fantasy, then, the early experience of academe was one primarily of exclusion. They were deemed juvenile and escapist, unworthy of criticism (Tallis 1984: 192), incapable of addressing themselves to important, real-life concerns (Tallis 1984: 192), impediments 'to the free operation of the reader's intelligence' (quote from Tallis 1984: 192, see also Horskotte 2004: 37), and easy to write (Tallis 1984: 207), nothing more than an author's 'self-indulgent catharsis' (Hunt 2001/2004 in Hunt and Lenz 2001/2001: 4, summarizing but not agreeing with views on fantasy) that required only passive engagement from readers (Tallis 1984: 192; Horskotte 2004: 37).

Attitudes began to change from about 1960 (Luckhurst 2005: 6; Wolfe 1986: xxii; Clareson 1971: xiv), prompted at least in part, it has been suggested, by the launch of *Extrapolation: A Science Fiction Newsletter* in 1959 (Luckhurst 2005: 9), the publication of Amis's *New Maps of Hell* in 1960 (Clareson 1971: xiv; Wolf 1986: xxviii), and the Ballantine paperback issue of Tolkien's *The Lord of the Rings* (Carter 1973: 118; Chadbourne 2008: 10; Sullivan 1996: 311; Wolfe 1986: xxi). While a few commentators complained of 'tokenism' (Clareson 1971: xiv; Le Guin 1989/1993: 3), the consensus view was that by the mid-1970s academic interest in science fiction and fantasy had taken off (Broderick 2003: 61; Irwin 1976: 96; Mobley 1973: 117; Wingrove 1979: 288; Wolfe 1986: xi). Wingrove (1979: 288) was pleased to report that science fiction was 'no longer a "crank" literature'; Irwin (1976) declared that the time of 'snobbery' had 'vanished' (96), and Mobley (1973) spoke of a 'steadily increasing following of readers and critics' (117). As Wolfe (1986) notes, scholarly organizations such as The Science Fiction Research Association (SFRA), The Science Fiction Foundation, and The International Association for the Fantastic in the Arts (IAFA) were established; a number of peer-reviewed academic journals joined *Extrapolation* (e.g. *Science Fiction Studies, Foundation, The Journal of the Fantastic in the Arts*, and *Mythlore*); histories were written (e.g. Aldiss 1973; Clarke 1979; Nicholls 1979 for sf; Carter 1973 and deCamp 1976 for fantasy); edited collections were compiled (Schlobin, ed. 1982 for fantasy; Bleiler, ed. 1982; Clareson, ed. 1971; Parrinder, ed. 1979 in sf); and particular writers and their work scrutinised in single author studies (Shippey 1982 on Tolkien; Mathews 1977, Griffin and Wingrove 1984; on Aldiss; De Bolt, ed. 1979 on LeGuin). In addition, greater space was given to science fiction and fantasy works and authors in literary histories and companions (McHale 1991: 308).

An essential element in the development of science fiction and fantasy studies was the appearance of what have since come to be regarded as landmark critical surveys (Amis 1960/1963; Ketterer 1974; Rose 1981; Scholes 1975; and Suvin 1979 for sf; and Hume 1984; Irwin 1976; Lewis 1961; Manlove 1975; Swinfen 1984; Timmerman 1983; Tolkien 1947/1964; and Wolfe 1982 for fantasy). These early studies, to be sure, had their faults. Many of them, as Luckhurst (2005: 9) and Hunt (in Hunt and Lenz 2001/2004: 10) have both noted, were defensive in tone and purpose, and betrayed a degree of self-doubt (Wolfe 1986: xxiii). Timmerman (1983), for instance, was concerned to show that fantasy was not just a 'sideshow' (2). Swinfen (1984) set out to defend the genre against the charge that it was inherently inferior to realist literature (11), and Shippey (1982) was determined to prove once and for all that Tolkien's fiction was deserving of literary merit (4). Both Amis (1960/1963: 169) and Scholes (1975: 40) took care to point out that while they read and enjoyed science fiction, they were not under any circumstances to be thought of as 'addicts'. Some accounts felt the need to hedge positive assessments with overstated criticism. Amis (1960/1963) observed that science fiction was a significant 'means of dramatising social enquiry' (63), but then noted almost immediately afterwards that it could still be 'vulgarly presumptuous' (63). He pointed to the genre's prophetic and visionary qualities (1960: 156), only to hurriedly assure any mainstream critics who might have been reading that this was 'the path which science fiction, in its faltering way, is just beginning to tread' (135). Wingrove (in Griffin and Wingrove 1984: xii) suggested that Aldiss could be compared to some of the great modernist writers, and then added, 'this is not to say that on the whole the quality of Aldiss's work matches that of Joyce or Kafka.' The comparison is made 'merely to emphasize the similarity in aims' (Wingrove, in Griffin and Wingrove 1984: xii). Irwin (1976: 183) proposed that fantasy, in the guise of play, asked readers to question the norms it seemed to uphold, but then muted this claim with a restatement of the establishment view, that the genre was inherently conservative and norm-affirming, thereby causing 'no lasting change in readers or society through readers' (Irwin 1976: 183). Swinfen (1984) very convincingly demonstrated that fantasy can be 'serious, effective and powerful', but then stepped away from her own argument to note that less successful fantasies 'would not be difficult to find' (97).

A number of these early studies tacitly accepted the prevailing view of science fiction and fantasy as generally poor by positioning their chosen works for study as rare and worthy exceptions. Scholes (1975) makes it clear from the start that he is dealing with only those authors who meet the highest standards (43). Writers 'deficient in their understanding of the cosmic structure', or who send 'men to

Mars merely to tell a cowboy story' (43), for example, are discounted. Suvin (1979) dismisses 'eighty to ninety percent' of science fiction as 'sheer confectionary' (36), and 'ninety or even ninety-five percent' of it as 'strictly perishable stuff' (vii). Manlove (1975) concludes that the fantasy authors he studied failed to live up to the terms of their own vision in their works, and so 'are best left to the cultists' (1975: 261). Hume (1984) sets out to reposition fantasy with respect to realism, but still asks why 'so much' of it is 'incontrovertibly trivial' (150). Other studies employed more positive strategies, pointing out that mainstream canon greats, from Shakespeare and Milton and Pope to Woolf and Pynchon and Atwood, turned to science fiction and fantasy when it suited them (Carter 1973: 16; Irwin 1976: 4–5, 186). A number of discussions, especially in fantasy (Hume 1984; Irwin 1976; Shippey 1982), imported Frye's (1975) framework of fictional modes as it allowed the genre to be defined in the aca- demically credible terms of myth and romance. Following a similar impulse, many scholars of fantasy claimed the genre as a primary form of literature by linking it to the oldest forms of human story- telling (Carter 1973: 12; de Camp 1976; Hume 1984: 21, 30; Manlove 1975; Swinfen 1984: 75; Thompson 1982). Hume (1984: 36) and Carter (1973: 3) both pointed out that the realist tradition arose in opposition to fantasy, which had dominated the production of literature for centuries (see also de Camp 1976: 7; Lewis 1961: 62).

These defensive impulses are, arguably, more about the critical atmosphere of the time than the texts themselves. As Luckhurst (2005) notes, they are more than likely 'driven by the need, under- standable in the nascent years of academic study of popular culture, to legitimate study of the genre to sceptical colleagues' (9). Defensive, inconsistent, and insecure though they sometimes were, these early studies nevertheless changed the face of criticism in science fiction and fantasy. They declared the realist approach to criticism unfit for purpose, put forward new frameworks of analysis and discussion, devel- oped genre definitions, carved out sub-genres, and established a canon of science fiction and fantasy classics (for 'sf', see Amis 1960/1963; Ketterer 1974; Russ 1975; Scholes 1975; and Suvin 1979; for fantasy, see Hume 1984; Irwin 1976; Lewis 1961; Manlove 1975; Swinfen 1984; Timmerman 1983; and Tolkien 1947/1964). A second wave of work soon appeared that both challenged and extended this pioneering material. Feminist (Attebery 1992; Lefanu 1988; Moody 2000; Wolmark 1994, 1986), Marxist (Moylan 1986), post-colonial (Alessio 2001; Inayatullah 2003; Kavanagh et al. 2001; Mandala 2008; Short 2004), and meta-textual (Attebery 1992) readings of these genres have widened existing avenues of interpretation and opened up new ones. The intersection with post-modernism has been particularly productive, and has often been credited with bringing science fiction and fantasy firmly and finally into the mainstream (Attebery 1992; 40; Hollinger and Gordon, eds. 2002; Luckhurst 2005; 10, 197; Manlove 1999: 2; McCaffery 1991; McHale 1991). The meeting of post-modernism and cyber-punk has excited particular interest. As McCaffery (1991) and Hollinger (1991) have noted, cyber-punk, with its often unforgiving explorations of the technologically enabled collapse of the human/machine binary, dovetails almost exactly with the post-modern perspective (see also Hollinger 2000; Hollinger and Gordon, eds. 2002; and Luckhurst 2005: 10, 197). Comments made by some of the post-modern critics are, perhaps, one of the most telling indicators of establishment credibility. Hollinger and Gordon (2002), for example, produce their collection in response to an 'sf canon' that they felt had become complacent, and their aim was to 'disrupt the potential ossification' they saw as imminent in the study of science fiction. A discipline has to be very comfortably situated indeed in order to be charged with complacency.

Science fiction and fantasy, once laughable non-subjects, are now at the centre of a thriving arena of academic debate (Stockwell 2000: 111). Traces of insecurity and self-doubt, of course, linger here and there. There is still a tendency to justify interest in the subject (Armitt 2005, 1996; Hunt and Lenz 2001/2004; Manlove 1999); canon greats are still claimed as genre authors (Armitt 2005: 15; Attebery 1992; 4; Manlove 1999: 36), and there are, surprisingly, still a number of complaints about exclusion from academe (Armitt 1996: 2; Attebery 1992; ix–x; Chadbourne 2008: 10; Luckhurst 2005; Manlove 1999: 3). I say 'surprisingly' here because there is now so much interest in, and so many studies on, science fiction and fantasy that complaints of exclusion are no longer sustainable. Histories, surveys and edited collections continue to appear (e.g. Aldiss and Wingrove 1986/2001;

Armitt 2005, 1996; Ashley 2005; James and Mendlesohn eds. 2003; Luckhurst 2005; Manlove 1999; Parrinder, ed. 2000; Roberts 2006/ 2001; Sawyer and Seed, eds. 2000; Seed, ed. 1995, 2004; Weldes, ed. 2003), as do single author studies (Chance and Sievers, eds. 2005 on Tolkien; Hunt 2001/2004 in Hunt and Lenz 2001/2004 on Le Guin and Pullman; Henighan 1999 on Aldiss; White 1999 on Le Guin; Schweitzer 1989 on Dunsany). Critical guides and reference tools are readily available (e.g. Clute and Grant 1997; Conley et al. 2006; James and Mendlesohn, eds. 2003; Wolfe 1986), and the mainstream quality press seems ever more willing to devote space to analytical features on science fiction and fantasy, as evident in the recent piece on fantasy in *The Telegraph Review* (12 April 2008), and the coverage of the re-made *Battlestar Galactica* in *The Guardian's G2* section (19 March 2009). In addition, science fiction and fantasy are firmly established in university curricula – in literature courses as well as in the more predictable film and cultural studies programmes – and are even now paving the way for serious consideration of a long-time poorer cousin, the graphic novel. Once derided as the province of the 'geek' fringe, science fiction and fantasy are now integral to the cultural landscape, 'part of the fabric of contemporary culture' (Wolfe 2002: 27, on fantasy), 'part of the cultural wallpaper' (Aldiss 2001: ii, on science fiction). Fantasy, as Wolfe (2002: 27) points out, is now nearly all pervasive, 'infiltrating other genres, the literary mainstream, otherwise conventional movies and TV programs, commercial art and advertising, music, theatre, design' (27). Stockwell (2003a) makes the same point for science fiction, noting that it 'informs the film and literature, the advertising and music, the street furniture and product design, food, fashion and language of global culture' (197).

The critical work on science and fiction and fantasy that has been progressing since the early 1960s has, in large part, made the re-evaluation of these genres from laughable to laudable possible by overturning many of the questionable assumptions that had accrued around them. It has been argued in several places, for example, that science fiction and fantasy are not to be dismissed as juvenile and escapist fluff. Drawing on Tolkien's arguments (1947/1964), Hunt (in Hunt and Lenz 2001/2004: 7) and Swinfen (1984: 54, 76) both note that fantasy is not, in fact, easy to write, but hard: in order to create compelling and convincing other worlds, insightful observations of the world as it is are necessary. It has also been shown that neither genre can depend on the shared reader-writer context often taken for granted in realist narratives (Attebery 1992: 132). In fantasy, 'there is no comfortable matrix of the commonplace to substitute for the imagination' (Le Guin 1989/1993: 3), and the writer cannot 'count on his reader's easy familiarity with what he is talking about' (Carter 1973: 175). Stockwell (2003b: 266) puts forward much the same case for science fiction, observing that a setting such as London in a realist novel can be sketched mostly in outline, as readers can be confidently left to fill in 'much of the rich detail' on their own. A writer like Stephen Baxter, on the other hand, has much more work to do in a novel such as *The Time Ships* (1995), which presents London as 'an overgrown, squalid and militarized 1930s city under a concrete dome that protects it from German bombs that have reigned down for the duration of the continuous war since 1914' (Stockwell 2003b: 267).

Fantasy especially was branded as being just for children, as Hunt (in Hunt and Lenz 2001/2004) has noted, and this assumption has also been vigorously challenged. In his groundbreaking work on the subject, Tolkien (1947/1964) noted that he could see nothing to justify the then commonly held belief that there was some 'natural connection between the minds of children and fairy-stories' (34). Children, he argued, did not like or dislike fantasy, or understand it any better, than they did anything else (34). Some would read it and take to it, others would not (35). The children who did like it, Tolkien (1947/1964) argued, were unlikely to simply grow out of it; rather, their appreciation for it would grow and mature as they did (35). Fantasy, as Sullivan (1996: 309) notes, tends to be read by 'all age groups', not just children. For Carter (1973), fantasy proper is not for children at all; for him, it is fiction for adults, 'a story which challenges the mind, which sets it *working*' (6).

The charge of escapism has been dealt with in a number of ways. Hume (1984: 81) notes that while fantasy may seem escapist at first glance, it is nevertheless significant since it indicates a fundamental dissatisfaction with the world as it is (81) and encourages a healthy belief in 'meaningful action' by individuals (68). Hunt (in Hunt and Lenz 2001/2004: 8), tilling ground prepared by Tolkien (1947/1964), notes that the charge of escapism is based on false assumptions, one being that escape is necessarily bad (see also Hume 1984: 81). For Tolkien (1947/1964), the element of escape in fantasy was entirely positive, and he explains this position by likening the citizen of the modern world to a prisoner. We are imprisoned, says Tolkien (1947/1964), not only by dehumanizing, ruinous technology – the 'noise, stench, ruthlessness, and extravagance of the internal combustion engine' – but also be the evils of a fallen world: 'hunger, thirst, poverty, pain, sorrow, injustice, death' (58). Any sane and rational person would seek escape from this, and fantasy provides that escape (Tolkien (1947/1964), not gratuitously, by simply allowing us a break from it all every now and again, but by reminding us of what is actually real (Tolkien 1947/1964, see also Le Guin 1974/1993: 40; Parker 1956: 601; Timmerman 1983: 56). In the daily world of lived experience, as Tolkien (1947/1964) explains, we are continually content to diminish ourselves by accepting a great many things as real that are not actually so. We will, he says, happily accept a swimming pool in place of the ocean, often without realizing what a compromise this is (63). Fantasy stories, says Tolkien, do not admit such compromises. They 'may invent monsters that fly the air or dwell in the deep, but at least do not try to escape from heaven or the sea' (Tolkien 1947/1964: 63).

Perhaps the most effective response to the charge of escapism has been the argument that science fiction and fantasy are not created to satisfy some fleeting whim (Stockwell 2003a: 198; Tolkien 1947/1964) but to challenge readers by interrogating what have become habitual and reflexive modes of thought. By dramatizing 'thought experiments' (Le Guin 1976/1993: 159; Macleod 2003: 31; Swinfen 1984: 231), science fiction and fantasy challenge accepted patterns of thinking (Amis 1960/1963: 156; Friend 1973: 1002; James 2003: 222; Ketterer 1974: 18; Meyers 1980: 209; Scholes 1975: 17; Seed 1999: 9; Suvin 1979). They prompt us to ask, for example, what if gender were irrelevant? (Le Guin 1976/1993: 159). What if the world as we know it were swept away in some catastrophe? (Amis 1960/1963; Hillegas 1971: 275). What if nuclear war were actually declared? (Seed 1999: 9).

What if secularism turns out not to be a good idea? (Shippey 1977: 161).

Fantasy's potential for stimulating new ways of thinking has also been articulated, although in a different way. In response to claims that it simply reinforces 'current ideologies' (Horskotte 2004: 37) or 'rarely challenges us to think' (Hume 1984: 81), a number of commentators have countered with Tolkien's (1947/1964: 48) recovery thesis, which states that fantasy, in creating a secondary world that strips away or warps what we have come to take for granted as real, reveals far more profound and fundamental truths (thus allowing us to 'recover' them). Effective fantasy removes the blinders imposed by the real world, allowing us to see it more clearly (Fredericks 1978: 7; Le Guin 1974/1993: 40; Parker 1956: 601; Swinfen 1984: 6; Timmerman 1983: 56; Wolfe 1986: xx). As Le Guin's (1974/1993: 40) articulation of this idea demonstrates, fantasy does not 'manipulate readers into passive acceptance' (see earlier discussion of the literary fantastic on page 3). It challenges them to look afresh at their lives, right down to the smallest details.

> For fantasy is true, of course. It isn't factual, but it is true. Children know that. Adults know it too, and that is precisely why many of them are afraid of fantasy. They know that its truth challenges, even threatens, all this false, all that is phony, unnecessary, and trivial in the life they have let themselves be forced into living. They are afraid of dragons because they are afraid of freedom. (Le Guin 1974/1993: 40)

Fantasy, once dismissed as a bit of silliness, has been re-evaluated as a literature of challenge, a genre that dares to suggest the systems and habits we call life may not be life at all.

Perhaps most significantly, the re-evaluation of science fiction and fantasy has revealed that these literatures are not divorced from real-world concerns and the complexities of the human condition, but fundamentally involved with them. The other worlds of science fiction and fantasy are interpreted as analogues of this one, and what happens there taken as a critique of what is happening here (Amis 1960/1963: 63; Hillegas 1971: 276; Hollinger and Gordon 2002: 4; Hunt in Hunt and Lenz 2001/2004: 8; Swinfen 1984: 2). As a number

of commentators have pointed out, the experiences of aliens, supernatural beings and humans in various kinds of other worlds serve to
explore our often troubled relationship with difference, be it racial
(Amis 1960/1963; Roberts 2006); sexual (LeFanu 1988; Moody 2000;
Roberts 2006; Wolmark 1994); religious (Mendlesohn 2003: 268), or
physical (see, for example, Robin Hobb's treatment of obesity in *The
Soldier Son Trilogy,* 2005–2007, and Stephen Donaldson's use of lep-
rosy in *Lord Foul's Bane,* 1977). It has also been noted that science
fiction and fantasy can be important barometers of various kinds of
social fear. Fantasy's 'supernatural terrors', as Parkinson (1987: 89)
notes, often represent actual terrors, such as the fear of social and
moral chaos (Zanger 1982: 230), the fear of evil (Drabble, ed. 2000:
351), and the fear of addiction, as Shippey (1982: 106) has argued
with reference to Gollum's need for the ring in *The Lord of the Rings,*
and Chadbourne (2008: 10) has suggested of Moorcock's Elric, who
depends on his demonically possessed sword in the same way an addict
does a drug. Auerbach (1997) analyses the sub-genre of vampire
fantasy fiction as a literature of social fear – the fear of the unknown,
the fear of losing control, the fear of disease, the fear of urban gangs.
Science fiction, of course, is frequently associated with fears relating to
the use of science and technology (Amis 1960/1963; Clarke 1979; Delany
1968/1977: 200; Hillegas 1971; Hollinger 1991; James 2003; Luckhurst
2005; McCaffery 1991; Roberts 2006; Rose 1981; Seed 2004), and this
concern, while less salient in fantasy, is far from absent. Tolkien
(1947/1964) himself professed a preference for castles over 'robot-
factories' (64) and his concerns over increasingly rampant industrial-
ization emerged, as Shippey (1982) observes, in *The Lord of the
Rings* (see also Tad Williams' science fantasy quartet *Otherland,* which
investigates the possibilities, both advantageous and dangerous, of
virtual reality). Fears relating to the threat of nuclear war have been
instanced in both genres, most notably by Seed (1999) with reference
to American science fiction of the Cold War era, but also Hoey (2000:
152) in connection with Moorcock's *The Eternal Champion.*

Science fiction and fantasy are not only considered worthy of criticism for the role they play in dissecting attitudes towards difference
and exposing social fears; they are also valued as significant arenas
of political and intellectual dissent. As Seed (1999:9) and Stockwell

(2003a: 198), both echoing Suvin (1979), have noted, science fiction
does not seek to passively reflect, but to transform (Suvin 1979: 10)
by active participation. While American science fiction prior to
the 1960s is often associated with celebrations of 'imperialistic and
militaristic glory' (Lefanu 1988:4), and xenophobic fears of invasion
(Seed 1999), commentators have pointed to a seam of work written
in apparent opposition to such themes. U/dystopian and feminist
science fiction and fantasy are analysed for the way they subvert
capitalist (Moylan 1986) and patriarchal power structures (Lefanu
1988; Wolmark 1994), and the post-colonial readings noted earlier
also present cogent critiques of imperialism. Earlier work on the
same trajectory can be found in Amis (1960/1963) and Hillegas
(1971). Consider as well that science fiction has been interpreted as
a platform for discussion of freedom and free will. Both Amis
(1960/1963) and Seed (2004), for example, read u/dystopian fiction
in relation to the rise of intolerant, totalitarian governments (see also
James 2003), and the fear of state-sponsored mind control. Amis
(1960/1963) also saw in science fiction a tendency to celebrate inde-
pendence and individuality (84). This emerges negatively in a range
of works that revealed humans to be no more than puppets of some
greater power, thus 'allegorising a fear of the loss of individuality and
free will' (Amis 1960/1963: 60–1), and positively in works that
applaud the 'maverick' as hero (Amis 1960/1963: 82).

Political commentary is no less evident in fantasy, particularly
with respect to the exercise of power (Mobley 1973; Shippey 1982;
Swinfen 1984; Thompson 1982). As Swinfen (1984: 20, 34, chapter 8)
repeatedly and at length points out, animal fantasies provide an
effective means of dramatizing political critique. Secondary world
fantasies, she further finds, deal with a number of weighty political
themes, such as 'problems of social structure and government', 'the
destructive nature of power – destructive both to those who wield it
and to those who are subject to it', and 'the self-destructive effects of
wealth and power and knowledge turned to the wrong ends' (Swinfen
1984: 96). In an entirely compatible analysis, Thompson (1982) points
out that fantasy, although often set in medieval or medieval-like times,
is nevertheless clearly concerned with issues of politics that 'retain a

special relevance to the modern era', such as 'the problems of power', and 'the conflict between individual freedom and social responsibility' (223). And while it is true that fantasy often illustrates ordered and hierarchical societies, this does not prevent the genre from engaging in political critique. As Zanger (1982: 230) points out, these supposedly rigid societies are often depicted at unstable times, either when they are just emerging, on the verge collapse, or undergoing some radical transformation.

Style: The Neglected Aspect

After some forty years of scholarship, we now have, to borrow Le Guin's (1977/1993: 130) terms 'theses, counter-theses, journals of criticism, books of theory, the big words'. No longer are science fiction and fantasy dismissed as juvenile and escapist nonsense that is easy to write, self-indulgent, unchallenging, and unworthy of study. Rather, the now impressive research record on these literatures convincingly demonstrates that they are often powerful instruments of social and political commentary, effective means of disruption and dissent, and, ultimately, significant tools for speculation on the very nature of reality. In one respect, however, this very notable body of research on science fiction and fantasy has failed: it has not significantly re-evaluated the issue of style. This is curious, since style, as writer/critics Delany (1969) and Le Guin (1979/1993) have noted, is essential. For Delany (1969), in fact, style is all there is, since content, he argues, does not actually exist (52); rather, it is nothing more than 'the illusion myriad stylistic features create when viewed from a distance' (54). Expressing the same view in a different metaphor, Le Guin (1979/1993) notes that

> many readers, many critics and most editors speak of style as if it were an ingredient of a book, like sugar in a cake, or something added on to a book, like frosting on the cake. The style, of course, *is* the book. If you remove the cake all you have left is a recipe. If you remove style all you have left is a synopsis of the plot. (Le Guin 1979/1993: 30)

Such calls to give style serious consideration in science fiction and fantasy have, however, largely gone unheeded. More often than not, style in these genres is dealt with in a knee-jerk fashion, assumed to be either plain and unexperimental – 'serviceable but inelegant', as Scholes (1975: 49) put it – or downright poor: clumsy, intrusive, and unconcerned with literary quality (for fantasy, see Attebery 2003, 1992; Chadbourne 2008; Hume 1984; Irwin 1976; Mobley 1973; Timmerman 1983: 5; for science fiction, see Amis 1960/1963; Hollinger 1991: 203; Roberts 2006: 42; Scholes 1975; Stockwell 2000; Taylor 1990). Part of the problem may be the long shadow cast by the pulps. Dated from c. 1920–1950, the pulp era refers to the explosion of science fiction and fantasy publishing in (primarily) American magazines such as Gernsback's *Amazing Stories* (Stockwell 2000: 76). The use of language in the pulps, or pulp style, as it is called, has been met with near-universal derision. Carter (1973) summarizes the view from fantasy, noting that

> from their inception the popular pulp fiction magazines in America specialised in swiftly moving, action-filled, easy-reading stories with a primary emphasis on entertainment value to the exclusion of literary quality. (Carter 1973: 49)

Amis's (1960/1963) comments on pulp science fiction run along the same lines. The magazine stories were popular and numerous, but stayed 'firmly at a humble level of literary endeavour' (38), showing 'a lack of subtlety and an almost imbecilic ignorance of, or indifference to, elementary literary pitfalls' (39). More bluntly, the pulps demonstrated 'stylistic imbecility' (Amis 1960/1963: 40). Pulp style did not experiment or innovate (Griffin and Wingrove 1984: xi; Attebery 2003: 41). It was 'weak' and 'awkwardly constructed' (Attebery 2003: 35), 'repulsive' (Amis 1960/1963: 40), 'crude' and 'unutterably poor' (Aldiss 2001: ix–x). Taylor (1990) and Stockwell (2000: 79–90) list a number of 'signature' pulp features, including intrusive and over-long passages of exposition; story titles that resemble newspaper headlines with their use of short and simple noun phrases (e.g. 'Big Game'); needless repetition of adjectives and adverbs that serve as little more than fillers; a dependence on third person omniscient narration; dialogue that is too complex syntactically to convincingly represent talk; and a tendency to use unnatural synonyms for the speech reporting verb 'said', and to modify those synonyms with equally unnatural adverbs (e.g. '*No!*', *he blustered roarily*).

From about the 1960s, a different trend in science fiction and fantasy writing, a 'new wave', came to the fore (Stockwell 2000: 76). 'New wave' science fiction and fantasy, was, among other things, characterized by thematic pessimism, an interest in subjective experience, and an increasing willingness to experiment with style (Broderick 2003; Luckhurst 2005; Roberts 2000: 81–2; Stockwell 2000:9; Taylor 1990: 619). As McHale (1991) has noted, the appearance of new wave work was one of the factors that led to the re-evaluation of science fiction and fantasy as detailed in the discussion above – it is surely no coincidence that academic interest in these genres picked up at about the same time as new wave work was beginning to have an impact. However, this only seems to have happened at the thematic level. With the recognition of 'textually innovative' work characterized by 'norm violating language' (McHale 1991: 313), one might have expected the barrage of complaints about poor style to be tempered with more balanced appraisals. This is not, however, what happens. Instead, two rather different reactions are more salient in the research record. Authors representative of or writing in the new wave style were either (1) accepted, but only as worthy exceptions; or (2) criticized for frivolous and self-indulgent stylistic experimentation. According to Stockwell (2000), for example, writers like Brian Aldiss (*Barefoot in the Head*), Margaret Atwood (*The Handmaid's Tale*) and Russell Hoban (*Riddley Walker*) are 'the avant-garde of science fiction', sought out by academics who value 'the unusual, the eccentric, unique and deviant', but not representative of the whole (Stockwell 2000: 76). Taylor's (1990) view was similar. While he found much of value in the new wave style, he suggested it would appeal mostly to the 'culturally literate', in contrast to the great mass of science fiction, which, he thought, would continue to address 'the lowest common denominator' (Taylor 1990: 619). Ketterer (1974), encountering stylistic experimentation in Aldiss's *Barefoot in the Head*, took the other critical route, positioning the work not as a worthy exception but as a failure, a linguistic indulgence emphasizing form at the expense of meaning (Ketterer 1974: 259).

Thus was the new wave's influence on style waved away. At best, it was considered something of a minor movement that produced a few texts of significance to analysts, critics, and the well-read, but was of questionable relevance more generally (Stockwell 2000: 76). At worst, it was considered to be not so much a wave but a 'ripple' (Del Ray 1979 in Taylor 1990: 612), a poor and late attempt at modernism (Griffin and Wingrove 1984: xx) that indulged in meaningless experiments with form. Style in science fiction and fantasy, it seems, has not been able to win. When it is not particularly experimental, it is criticized for a lack of innovation; when it does present linguistic experimentation, it is criticized for taking it too far for no important reason.

For a number of commentators, the greater bulk of science fiction and fantasy remains as 'pulpy' as ever. Roberts (2006: 12), for example, supposes that there may be sf texts that have 'beautiful or experimental writing styles', but then immediately says 'most do not' (12). For Stockwell (2000: 102), departures from pulp in science fiction 'are exceptions rather than the rule'. While science fiction is experimental in most other respects – 'breaking and rewriting the laws of physics, moving planets, travelling through time and questioning the nature of matter and existence' (Stockwell 2000: 50) – it is, he claims, still plain and unremarkable in terms of style (51, 102). According to Hollinger (1991), most science fiction still relies on 'transparency of language' (203). Comments on style in fantasy are similar, with a number writers (e.g. Attebery 1992; Chadbourne 2008; Irwin 1976; Timmerman 1983) suggesting that the language of the genre avoids complexity, tending instead towards staid, unadorned prose. 'Well-crafted words', claims Chadbourne (2008: 10), 'are for literary texts' – fantasy has other concerns. For Irwin (1976), fantasy is by definition stylistically plain: works of fiction that are linguistically experimental may qualify as some other kind of imaginative literature, but simply are not fantasy.

While great strides have been made in re-evaluating science fiction and fantasy in terms of theme and socio-political significance, stylistic value, especially with regard to experimentation and innovation, are still, it seems considered something of a rarity in these genres. Interestingly, many sources, while keen to insist that style in science fiction and fantasy is mostly poor or unremarkable, are somewhat less keen to present solid evidence for this view. Amis (1960/1963), for example, knows that he finds style in science fiction to be amateurish, but he really cannot say why. He quotes a snatch out of 'The Monster from Nowhere' (1935) in support of his views, but he does not specify what elements in the passage make the prose so execrable. Apparently, this is supposed to be self evident. The only hint he gives is to complain that the monsters are referred to with the relatively weak word 'thing', but even this seems unwarranted, as the monsters are described in other ways, too, for example, 'huge amorphous blobs of jet black, which seemed to be of the earth, yet not quite of it' ('The Monster from Nowhere', in Amis 1960/1963: 39). Amis (1960/1963: 40–3) cites other passages from other stories and does give details as to why he finds them poor, but these details tend to focus on content rather than style. Roberts (2006), who conceded that most science fiction texts probably lack 'beautiful or experimental writing styles' (12), actually spends very little time on style, focusing instead on why science fiction is of socio-cultural importance in chapters on race, gender and technology. Mobley (1973: 127) accepts that style in fantasy is often weak, but this assessment does not seem to be based on any considered analysis of style. She suggests, for example, that fantasy exhibits stylistic extravagance, and offers as evidence the frequent use of hyperbolic comparative structures such as 'more horrible than can be imagined' (124). However, she gives only two examples, which does not establish frequency, and why should such structures necessarily be considered weaknesses in any case? This question is left unconsidered in Mobley's (1973) account.

Rather than give evidence for stylistic naivety, or question that assumption in the first place, the more usual pattern in studies of science fiction and fantasy is for commentators, even those seeking to defend these genres, to accept the view that style is weak or uninspiring, and set about explaining why is it should be excused. A number of studies, for example, grant that style is a weak point, but go on to argue that this is excusable because it is the content – the ideas and the story – that really matter (Amis 1960/1963: 118;

Chadbourne 2008: 10; Roberts 2006: 12; Scholes 1975: 78; Stockwell 2003b: 255, 2000: 102; Timmerman 1983: 5). Science fiction and fantasy are also excused for their allegedly poor style on the grounds that they have the more important matter of myth to attend to (Aldiss and Wingrove 1986/2001: 4; Hillegas 1971; Hume 1984; Lewis 1961: 43, 46; Mobley 1973; Timmerman 1983). *Myth* in this context, particularly as concerns fantasy fiction, refers not to a story about the doings of gods and goddesses in ancient cultures, but to a more fundamental kind of story, a story with a capital 'S' that helps us understand the world and our place in it. As Armstrong (2005) notes, human intelligence is part rational and part intuitive. These two kinds of perception are different, but complementary, and we need both (Armstrong 2005). Reason, logic, and empirical observation feed our need for rational understanding, and myth takes over when these fail (Armstrong 2005). Hume (1984) explains it this way:

> [R]eason can only deal with the material universe, and few people get enough intensity or assurance from that to find scientific truth an entirely satisfactory frame of meaning. (Hume 1984: 196)

Science satisfies the rational half of our mind. It tells us how rainbows work. Myth serves the intuitive, emotional half. It tells us why we feel excited to behold them.

Articulating the view held by a number of others (e.g. Hume 1984; Mobely 1973), Timmerman (1983) suggests that fantasy fiction 'is a kind of myth' (28). It is especially important in our time, he suggests, because it

> stands in opposition to the iron-clad pragmatism of the age, and seeks to return man to a sense of origins and divine significance. (Timmerman 1983: 28)

This 'mythic dimension' (Mobley 1973: 124) is often invoked when excusing fantasy for poor style. While the 'fantasy as myth' thesis is convincing, the 'style in fantasy is poor but that is okay because it serves myth' thesis is less so. Mobley (1973), for example, declares that 'craft is secondary to the material' (126) in fantasy, and goes on to assert that even sword and sorcery, which is, according to her, particularly poor in style, can still be effective because (1) it meets the criteria for myth (126); and (2) myth is sufficiently robust 'to survive even mediocre retelling' (127). While Mobley (1973) makes a good case for the mythic in fantasy, her account does not establish the poverty of style that it asserts.

So strong is the commitment to the 'style is poor' mantra in studies of science fiction and fantasy that evidence to the contrary is sometimes downplayed, reported with seeming reluctance. Scholes (1975), for instance, cites and analyses instances of effective and evocative style in several texts (Keyes' *Flowers for Algernon*, Sturgeon's 'Slow Sculpture' and Stapledon's *Star Maker*), and speaks encouragingly about writers 'trying to extend' the stylistic horizons of science fiction and fantasy, 'in some cases with considerable success' (1975: 49). By way of conclusion, however, he retreats from his own analysis in order to maintain the status quo regarding weakness of style:

[A]nd here, though admitting that in the world of structural fabulation [his term for science fiction] ideas take precedence over their verbal formulae, I tried to indicate that writers like Sturgeon, Keyes, and Stapledon himself use language with a care and precision that is more than functional and approaches beauty. (Scholes 1975: 78)

Scholes's (1975) work on these texts is sufficiently rigorous and convinces in its own right: the case for care, precision, and beauty in the use of language was made. The opportunity to overtly challenge the notion that 'ideas take precedence over their verbal formulae', however, was not taken. Irwin (1976) is so committed to the thesis that language in fantasy is straightforward and unexperimental that he brushes aside the widespread use of neologism, asserting that it is 'rarely found' (79), when, in fact, it is commonly found. Carter (1973), for example, devotes an entire chapter to coining new terms in fantasy, and notes that the most effective fantasies develop and maintain extensive vocabularies of coined terms. While Irwin (1976) could not ignore Tolkien in his discussion, he dismissed his use of neologism as minor and 'mostly used in place names' (80). Such an assessment is difficult to interpret when set against Tolkien's creation of languages, let alone coined terms.

The critical world, happy enough to re-evaluate science fiction and fantasy in terms of theme, message and significance, seems stubbornly committed to the thesis that style in these genres is not up to much, even in the face of evidence to the contrary. The question that arises, of course, is why. Why do studies of science fiction and fantasy cling so tenaciously to the belief that style in science fiction and fantasy is as a rule either barely adequate or distractingly poor? Why should this assumption be so seldom questioned or challenged? One reason may be to do with the way that language, the vehicle of style, is often dealt with in critical enquiries of these genres. While there is some evidence of insightful work on language in literary-critical studies of science fiction and fantasy, such as Hollinger's (2000) account of first person narration and the illusion of a fixed, discrete subject, this body of work has, in the main, suffered from various problems when looking at language, and this has impeded progress on the study of style. In a number of accounts, for example, there is a tendency to talk in general terms about the language of the text as though this were the same as analysing it. Taylor (1990) pointed to this tendency in the critical writings of Bainbridge, Aldiss and Blish, where 'generalized comments' about style occurred without 'specific devices or patterns' to support them (165). Dawson (2005) has proceeded in a similar way. Writing on *The Lord of the Rings*, she states that Middle-Earth is multilingual and multicultural and suggests that

> the ability and willingness to communicate with other ethnic and linguistic groups is an important trait of most of the inhabitants of Middle-Earth, and the key factor in the ultimate defeat of Sauron by the free-peoples. (Dawson 2005: 117)

While all of this sounds promising in terms of linguistic analysis, examples of these many languages do not substantiate the general comments, and neither is there any instanced discussion of character communication. This means that the potentially interesting point about language being a 'key factor in the ultimate defeat of Sauron' remains unexplored. Manlove (1975) cites a passage from C. S. Lewis's *Perelandra (Voyage to Venus)* that describes how the floating islands on the planet move with motion of the waves. While he initially indicates a linguistic analysis with the observation that 'the syntax brings the picture to life' (122), he does not follow through on this. *What* in the syntax animates the description? This question needs to be answered if the effective use of language in the passage is to be understood. McHale (1991) suggests that writers such as Heinlein, Asimov, Clarke and Sturgeon 'modelled their prose style and narrative structures on those of best seller fiction' (313), but provides no textual analysis in support of his view, making his claims difficult to evaluate. Moody (2000), writing with an explicitly declared interest in 'silence and language creation in women's science fiction' (179) observes that 'at the beginning of the novels [she studies] women are rendered silent or knowingly speak a language which is not their own' (182), and then goes to suggest that the women 'exist as a dispossessed or subjugated indigenous population' (182). But what are these languages that are not the women's own? How are they indicated in the text? And how is the language of the text linked to the themes of dispossession and subjugation? When speaking about language creation, Moody (2000) offers little in the way of textual analysis. Apart from instancing a few 'words and expressions' (Moody 2000: 181), she does not discuss these languages in detail, preferring instead to cite passages in which they are spoken about (e.g. Moody 2000: 183). Talking about language or citing characters who talk about it without analysing examples weakens the status of the conclusions drawn.

Cheyne (2006) and Lenz (in Hunt and Lenz 2001/2004) both notice the importance of language in Le Guin's fiction, but talk in general terms about language and leave it that. Cheyne's (2006) interest, for example, is translation in Le Guin's fiction, but her analysis does not really offer any insights into the language of the texts. Instead, she cites multiple examples of characters talking about translation and miscommunication rather than analysing the language *of* those miscommunications. Lenz (in Hunt and Lenz 2001/2004), looking at the *Earthsea* trilogy, states that the islanders generally speak Hardic, notes that this is derived from dragon speech, and points to the exceptions of the Kargard Empire and Osskil, 'whose eccentricity of language emphasizes their isolation' (45). The textual representation of these languages, however, is not of interest in her discussion, and the point about language and isolation is not substantiated. What, for example, makes the language of the Kargard Empire and Osskil 'eccentric'? Questions such as this are not posed or answered in Lenz's (in Hunt and Lenz 2001/2004) work. Instead, the account moves on to talk about issues of race, ethnicity and governance in the story. Swinfen (1984: 87) notices the same things about the different languages in *Earthsea* that Lenz (in Hunt and Lenz 2001/2004) does, but once again, a valid point about stylistic complexity is approached but not fully realized, as Swinfen (1984) does not take the next step – analysing the representation of the languages imagined for the secondary world. Swinfen (1984) is similarly vague when it comes to language in other texts. Speaking of Lloyd Alexander's *The Chronicles of Prydain*, she notes that 'the inhabitants of Prydain all speak one language, although the language of spells and enchantments is different, and important inscriptions are in the Old Writing' (85). However, she provides no actual linguistic analysis in support of these claims. *How* is the language of magic 'different'? What is the 'Old Writing'? How are they differentiated from the speech of the characters? Questions such as these, which would open the door to a closer examination of style, are not asked.

A number of literary accounts can also betray confusion and contradiction when it comes to the study of style. Attebery (1992), for example, has some very good things to say about style in fantasy. With reference to some of Gene Wolfe's work (*Book of the New Sun* and *The Urth of the New Sun*), he observes how Latinate words 'simultaneously suggest the Latin vocabulary of science and the Latin vocabulary of Medieval church, court, and coven' (124). However, he seems to negate such cogent observations by accepting as true the view that works of fantasy tends to be 'naive or artless because they emphasize story over verbal texture' (54). Manlove (1975) presents some very compelling stylistic analysis in *The Lord of the Rings* (his account of how Mordor is described convinces, for example), but still concludes that Tolkien's style was overall 'weak and bloodless' (206).

Compounding problems due to lack of evidence is the tendency to offer subjective opinions in place of linguistic analysis. James Branch

Cabell has 'a sophisticated prose style' (Carter 1973: 44), while MacDonald in *Phantastes* is 'discordant', sometimes '"purple" and highly emotive', sometimes 'forensic and pompous' (Manlove 1975: 78). Cordwainer Smith uses an 'odd lilting language' when describing visions (Attebery 2003: 44); Robert E. Howard 'wrote vivid, colourful stories of terrific verve and gusto', while Tolkien was rather more 'pedestrian' (Carter 1973: 63, 121). Stephen Donaldson distinguished himself with 'the ease' of his prose style and the 'fluidity and grace' of his writing (Timmerman 1983: 113). Tolkien's style in *The Hobbit* was for Swinfen (1984: 99) 'painfully avuncular', while Le Guin's was 'rhythmic but unadorned' (99). Sophisticated? Forensic? Avuncular? Lilting? Gusto? Ease? While all of these terms indicate some sort of intuitive reaction to the style of a particular text, they are far too subjective to be of use in a discussion of the way language and theme interact. These are, more than anything else, personal opinions, and while they are perfectly legitimate *as* opinions they do not serve to advance knowledge about style. When Carter (1973: 30) tells us Dunsany is 'a writer of incomparable style', and Timmerman (1983: 113) says he is given to 'poetic flights of fancy', we still know very little about Dunsany's use of language. When Hume (1984) declares that *Watership Down* simply lets the rabbit language 'substitute for real strangeness' and Swinfen (1984) declares with equal certainty that it 'is used so naturally that one almost expects documentary evidence for it' (39), we can conclude very little about style in Richard Adams' animal fantasy. When Attebery (2003: 34) simply states without evidence that there has been an improvement in 'the level of sophistication and stylistic distinction' between E. E. Doctorow Smith's fiction in the 1920s and Cordwainer Smith's in the 1950s, we are no further along in our understanding of style.

Also problematic in a number of attempts to look at style in science fiction and fantasy is the inclination to rely on popular notions about language, or to uncritically employ theoretical models of language. Hollinger (2002), for example, makes a distinction between 'middle-class English' and 'teenage slang' in a discussion of *A Clockwork Orange* and *Random Acts of Senseless Violence*, but unhelpfully assumes a somewhat simplistic relationship between class and dialect. Similar readings emerge when Bernstein's restricted code argument is uncritically applied. Bernstein (1966) argued that children from economically deprived backgrounds could also be linguistically deprived. He suggested that many of these children acquired a 'restricted' form of their language at home (e.g. fewer and more basic vocabulary items, less exposure to complex subordination and grammatically complete structures) and that this left them at a disadvantage at school. Bernstein's arguments, while robustly criticized on linguistic grounds (e.g. see Labov 1972), sometimes inform literary-critical studies of language in science fiction and fantasy. Clarke (1979), for example, talks about Nadsat speakers in Burgess's *A Clockwork Orange* in terms of 'linguistic disadvantage', claiming that they 'are confined by their circumstances to a restricted and predictable code that cannot find any words to express concepts' (274). While Alex in *A Clockwork Orange* may be a violent delinquent, it is clear that he is also articulate. Notice, for example, that he can style shift fluently and without hesitation. In the narration of his thoughts, he tends to use Nadsat: 'I could feel the knives in the old moloko starting to prick and now I was ready for a bit of the twenty-to-one' (Burgess 1962/1996: 7). When addressing a victim, he switches to standard English: 'It would interest me greatly, brother, if you would kindly allow me to see what books those are that you have under your arm' (1962/1996: 8). Here, Alex not only switches to standard English, but strategically uses situationally inappropriate politeness (Brown and Levinson 1978/ 1987) to mock his victim. In dismissing speakers of Nadsat like Alex as users of a 'restricted' code that 'cannot find any words to express concepts', Clarke (1979) has missed features of stylistic complexity in the text that are not only evident, but have a bearing on interpretation.

An uncritical acceptance of the Sapir-Whorfian view of language has also clouded views on style in science fiction and fantasy (see, for example, Broderick 2003; Cheyne 2006; Clarke 1979; Collings 1986). The Sapir-Whorf hypothesis states that language constrains perception, influencing how speakers observe the world. In its strongest version, the hypothesis suggests that language controls perception (see Crystal 1991: 297; Meyers 1980: 161). While this idea has had great popular appeal, it tends, as Meyers (1980: 169) has pointed out, to be treated with more caution among linguists, and it is perhaps for this reason that fiction centred on Sapir-Whorfian ideas, the most famous example of which is probably Orwell's *Nineteen Eighty-Four* (Stockwell 2000: 54), tends to be found less convincing when analysed linguistically. While Stockwell (2000: 55) has time for Newspeak as 'a prime example of science fictional commentary on language', he also points out that it presents a 'folk-linguistic view of how language works' and betrays the naive assumption that a language is only its words. Meyers' (1980: 33) take on *Nineteen Eighty-Four* is similar. Once the central premise – that language controls thought and perception – is dismissed from the analysis of Newspeak, what remains is, linguistically, not as impressive as it may first have seemed. Meyers (1980: 33) is more impressed by David Karp's *One*. In this work, citizens no longer conceive of themselves as individuals, and so refer to themselves in the third person. As a result, the first person pronouns are no longer used. Because this depicted fictional change has actual historical precedent[1] and involves the linguistic sub-system of pronouns rather than just words, Meyers (1980) finds it more believable: 'Newspeak, with the whole Ministry of Truth behind it, seems not as effective nor nearly as feasible a means of thought control as the simple changes of pronouns Karp depicts' (33). The uncritical acceptance of Sapir-Whorfism in literary-critical work on alternative world fiction has perhaps led to the privileging of some texts at the expense of others that may be equally worthy.

While literary-critical treatments of language in science fiction and fantasy are often marred by various conceptual and methodological weaknesses, linguistic treatments of these genres that are uninterested in them as literary art are also problematic. Meyers (1980), for example, concentrates mostly on the issue of scientific authenticity. While he notes that 'only science fiction requires its practitioners to put down on paper their estimates of the language of the next decade, the next century, or the next millennium' (1980: 12), he himself takes a relatively limited approach to these 'estimates' by asking only one question: do authors who are thematically interested in the theme of communication show sufficient knowledge of linguistic theory in their work? If they do, their work is deemed good, if they do not, it is deemed poor (most do not). Wider questions concerning relationships between language, character and theme are pushed aside.

And since, as Stockwell (2000: 48) notes, 'poor linguistic knowledge is no bar to producing interesting and poetic writing', Meyers (1980) misses the chance to look at some potentially interesting uses of language in the texts he finds lacking in theoretical sophistication.

Linguistic accounts can also adopt a literature-as-data rather than a literature-as-art approach. This occurs to some extent in Rey (2001), who does some interesting work on language and gender in the *Star Trek* franchise. The analysis, however, contributes primarily to cultural theory and less to our understanding of *Star Trek* as science fiction. The fictional dialogue is not investigated as an element in the drama, but as evidence of cultural attitudes towards gender roles. Levorato (2003), also interested in gender, takes a detailed look at the language of fairy tales (various versions of *Little Red Riding Hood*), but is primarily interested in how the language of the tales reflects ideological stances.

Stockwell's (2003a; 2003b; 2000) treatments, while rigorous and thorough linguistically, seem to offer divided accounts of style aesthetically. On the one hand, he sees great value in how science fiction uses language. It 'can do some discoursal things that no other form of literature can do' (2003a: 195), 'it often stretches the possibilities of literary organization beyond the limits of naturalistic fiction (2003a: 196), and it exhibits 'unique and innovative stylistic patterns and narratological techniques' (2003a: 196). Much of his own work supports these claims (see, for example, the analysis of metaphor in chapter 8 of *The Poetics of Science Fiction*), and a number of his analyses inform the work undertaken here. On the other hand, as noted earlier, he also declares that style in science fiction is, with only few exceptions, unimpressive and uninteresting. It 'has traditionally been very pedestrian, conservative, unimaginative and unspectacular' (2000: 50) and remains so. 'Science fictional prose is stereotypically blandly descriptive to the point of banality' (2000: 50), a pattern disturbed only 'the hyperbole of "Gosh-wow!" awe and wonder' (2000: 50). He further says that 'the vast majority of science fictional writing is not syntactically deviant or semantically challenging' (2000: 76); that most of it has 'retained the conventional pattern of fantastic content with prosaic delivery' (2000: 102); and that it is at best characterized by 'general invisible competence' (2000: 76), at worst by 'in-your-face-ineptitude' (2000: 76).

In contrast to other aspects of these genres, such as theme and socio-political significance, the study of style in science fiction and fantasy has stagnated. Literary-critical studies tend to offer unsubstantiated generalizations, subjective opinions, and flawed analyses based on the uncritical acceptance of controversial theoretical models. Linguistic treatments can analyse literary language as data and contribute to non-literary disciplines. Both approaches tend to betray confused positions on style, with insistent declarations of its general poverty sitting incongruously beside demonstrations of its effectiveness. Clearly it is time to reassess the issue of style in science fiction and fantasy. This book offers just such a reassessment by opening up the debate on style in these genres. It challenges the often-made claim that style in science fiction and fantasy is on the whole weak, plain, and dismissible by showing, in a series of literary stylistic analyses, how style is linked to two elements fundamental in both genres: the process of estrangement, and the construction of plausible other words.

Estrangement, as Stockwell (2000: 61) notes, is Suvin's (1979) articulation of what is also called *defamiliarization*. The basic principle is that a piece of art works by making the familiar strange so that an audience can see and reflect on features or circumstances that are typically taken for granted, and so would otherwise go unnoticed. For Suvin (1979), estrangement was an essential aspect of science fiction and he argued that the familiar was made strange in the genre primarily through a *novum*, 'a strange newness' (Suvin 1979). The nova are not, he says, such things as the gadgets in a James Bond film, but 'hegemonic' (70) and 'totalising' (64) phenomena that signal the world in the text is radically altered from the reader's own. To cite some very well known examples, nova are kings that get pregnant (Le Guin's *The Left Hand of Darkness*); teleportation technology (*Star Trek*), and firemen who start fires by profession rather than put them out (Bradbury's *Fahrenheit 451*). Such differences between our world and the fictional other world, as Hillegas (1971: 277) points out 'can be at heart distortions, inversions, and exaggerations of characteristics of

our own world'. In encountering them, 'the reader gains new understanding of life on our world' (277).

A defining aspect of science fiction as far as Suvin (1979) was
concerned, estrangement has nevertheless been invoked for fantasy,
as well. Attebery (1992), for example, connects estrangement with
fantasy's capacity to evoke wonder:

> [T]he concept of wonder, as a key to fantasy's impact, may be
> best understood as an alternative formulation of the idea of
> estrangement. (Attebery 1992: 16)

Fantasy, as Tolkien (1947/1964: 48) argued, presents readers with an
'arresting strangeness' (48) at odds with what they assume is real,
and in doing so prompts them to look at reality in a new way.
It 'provides the novelty that circumvents automatic responses and
cracks the crust of *habitude*' (Hume 1984: 196).

While for Suvin (1979) the issues were political and for Tolkien
(1947/1964) spiritual (Attebery 1992: 16), 'the strange newness'
(Suvin 1979: 4) in science fiction and the 'arresting strangeness'
(Tolkien 1947/1964: 48) in fantasy are both instruments of estrangement that prompt comparison between the world we know and the
world created in the text. The other worlds of science fiction and
fantasy, whether futuristic, pre-industrial, alternative or magical, all
take familiar aspects of our world and make them strange so that we
can, as Stockwell (2000: 146) puts it, re-cognize them.

For the process of estrangement to be effective, however, a careful
balance must be struck. The other world has to be different enough
so that the familiar does indeed become strange, but it cannot be so
different that it becomes impenetrable (Myers 1983; Stockwell 2000;
Sullivan 1996: 305). That this careful balancing act can be effectively
maintained linguistically in science fiction and fantasy has to date
been recognized only infrequently, and applied to only a small number
of texts. Myers' (1983) analysis, for example, convincingly demonstrates that balanced estrangement in science fiction can rest largely
on style. The language of the text, she suggests, must be different
enough from the reader's ordinary language to suggest otherness,
but near enough to still be understood, and authors have to find

a way to 'erect convincing barriers to communication' while still using 'predominantly the language of the audience' (Myers 1983: 306). Stockwell (2000, 1991) makes a similar point, and looks at how linguistically deviant texts train their readers in the 'new' language as they go. While these studies usefully and systematically demonstrate a clear link between style and effective estrangement, they are unfortunately not typical of the wider body of work on style in science fiction and fantasy, which, as noted earlier, tends to maintain that style in these genres is generally poor.

As Swinfen (1984: 234) has noted, fantasy has not only to make 'the familiar strange', but must also make 'the strange familiar'. This is a significant issue in both genres. As studies of science fiction and fantasy have shown over and over again, a central concern for both genres is the creation of plausible and compelling other worlds substantially removed from our 'primary' (Tolkien 1947/1964: 37) or 'zero' (Suvin 1979: 1) world (Amis 1960/1963; Fredericks 1978; Irwin 1976; Le Guin 1979/1993; Meyers 1980; Moylan 1986; Parker 1956; Roberts 2006; Stockwell 2000; Sullivan 1996; Swinfen 1984; Thompson 1982). The fantasy author 'should do *everything possible* to convince his reader that his invented world is real and genuine' (Carter 1973: 180), and the science fiction writer has to somehow present all that is innovated and extrapolated in a way that convinces (Bradbury 1968, cited in Stockwell 1991: 107). Discussions of other-world creation typically concentrate on features of content that enhance believability, such as the presentation of consistent geographies, histories, political structures and cultural elements (Carter 1973; Swinfen 1984; Thompson 1982: 223). Suvin (1979), Amis (1960/1963), and Roberts (2006) emphasize rational extrapolation from what is known, and Carter (1973), Swinfen (1984) and Roberts (2006) all note the importance of credibility-enhancing details. Less often noticed, however, is the extent to which the believability of the created world may rest on style. Other worlds in fiction are, after all, created from language, so it is reasonable to assume that style is integral to this endeavour. While the fundamental role that style can play in the creation of believable otherworlds is sometimes acknowledged (e.g. see Halliday 1973; Myers 1983; Shippey 1982), many discussions of this issue tend to be limited in various ways. Swinfen (1984: 85),

for example, states that secondary world fantasies can make themselves more convincing by positing their own distinct literatures
and languages, but offers no detailed analyses of these supposed
languages. Manlove (1975: 12) puts believability at the very centre
of his account, tasking himself with demonstrating whether or not
authors have created convincing secondary worlds. However, he often
applies a biographical approach that does not allow him to address
his own question. He says, for example, that it is in *The Water Babies*
that Kingsley 'comes nearest to finding himself' (17). While this may
or may not be so, it is difficult to see how this sheds light on whether
or not Kingsley has drawn a believable secondary world in his work.
While Manlove (1975) makes some interesting observations about
the use of narratorial intrusions in Kingsley's work, he uses this evidence in support of an argument about the emergence of Kingsley's
personality in his fiction (29). Again, this says more about the author
(or what Manlove thinks about him) than the believability of the
secondary world created. Manlove (1975) does move on to territory
nearer his question when he talks about a passage that reflects 'something of the roughness of life itself' (29), but the evidence he gives in
support of this is at the level of content rather than style.

Hume (1984) finds herself impressed with the secondary world
created in Golding's *The Inheritors*. 'What starts', she says, 'as a simple
challenge to our understanding when we enter his pattern of perception becomes an exciting new view of social relationships and of the
world' (Hume 1984: 135). As Halliday (1973) has shown, such effects
are achieved largely through the language of the text. On this issue,
though, Hume's (1984) account becomes confusing. Rhetorically,
her stance on language is informed by post-structuralism. According
to this view, the entire linguistic system is akin to one of those unhelpful dictionary definitions, where the defining terms of a word are just
as unclear as the unknown word itself, and so more words have to be
looked up, leading to more unhelpful definitions, and so on (Eagleton
1983). In accepting post-structuralist ideas about language, Hume
(1984) commits herself to several propositions: that 'texts cannot
describe reality, and indeed mostly refer to other linguistic conventions'
(5); that language is a largely flawed, unstable tool of communication
(132); and that words, because of their mutability in context, cannot

be said to mean anything (132). However, if language truly could not 'mean', if it could refer to nothing beyond itself, if communication were as vulnerable as post-structuralist thinking suggests, there would be nothing in *The Inheritors* to impress Hume (1984). There would be no *The Inheritors*. While Hume (1984) makes what is a very important point about style and the creation of plausible other worlds, that 'an author can reach a new kind of reality by manipulating language' (166), it emerges in a discussion informed by a theoretical stance on language that does not technically allow it to be concluded. It is time to look afresh at the role style can play in creating the other worlds so central to science fiction and fantasy, to move beyond assumptions, excuses and confused approaches into a considered exploration of the way language can be used to create convincing other worlds. As Delany (1969: 66) has said, 'any serious discussion of speculative fiction must get away from the distracting concept of sf content and examine precisely what sort of word-beast sits before us'.

Conclusion

While otherworld construction and estrangement are acknowledged as important aspects of science fiction and fantasy, style's potential contribution to their realization has thus far been given only cursory treatment. This has allowed the notion that style is adequate at best and poor at worst in these genres to circulate as accepted fact without serious challenge, leaving a significant gap in the research record. The remaining chapters of this book take the study of science fiction and fantasy in a new direction by addressing this gap, looking afresh at the much-maligned but much-misunderstood issue of style. Chapters 2 and 3 address the often-made claim that science fiction and fantasy avoid experiments in form by looking at texts that clearly do experiment in this way. The role of style in balancing linguistic estrangement with comprehensibility is considered with respect to innovative representations of future Englishes in Chapter 2, and challenging representations of past Englishes in Chapter 3. Chapters 4 and 5 concentrate on the so-called 'plain' language of science fiction and fantasy. Chapter 4 demonstrates that language which at first

glance seems pedestrian is nevertheless stylistically effective in presenting otherworlds that are physically, culturally and emotionally
convincing. Chapter 5 continues the exploration of supposedly plain
language by looking at one of its greatest but perhaps least acknowledged contributions to the creation of otherworlds in science fiction
and fantasy – the construction of compelling characters.

The analyses undertaken in each chapter, literary-stylistic in
approach, proceed by applying linguistic methods and frameworks to
the language of the texts in order to further our understanding of
them as literature. The frameworks used are explained as they arise,
although readers unfamiliar with them may wish to consult the given
references as well. The analytical units used include the traditional
grammatical categories, such as noun phrases, verb phrases and
voice, as well as more social categories of language analysis, such as
talk exchanges. While I began this chapter by defining science fiction
and fantasy separately, I will from this point collapse the distinction
between them. This may at first seem an odd decision since the two
genres are traditionally contrasted, science fiction considered the
literature of what might be, and fantasy the literature of what never
can be (Amis 1960/1963: 22; Hunt, in Hunt and Lenz 2001/2004: 12;
Irwin 1976: 96–7; Manlove 1975: 3, 1982: 18; Mobley 1973: 117;
Roberts 2006/2001: 5; Stockwell 2003b: 254–5; Suvin 1979: 101;
Swinfen 1984: 5). In some cases, the division has been vehemently
maintained. Suvin (1979) described fantasy as a 'rampantly socio-
pathological phenomenon' (9), and Amis (1960/1963) suggested 'that
a good look through the mailing lists of fantasy magazines would
amply repay anybody setting up in business as an analyst' (158). Such
assessments, however, are more a feature of the early days of science
fiction and fantasy criticism when definitions and boundaries where
important to establish. Since then, generic boundaries in general, and
the boundaries between science fiction and fantasy in particular, have
been called into question (Aldiss and Wingrove 1986/2001: 159–60;
Armitt 1996; Hollinger 2002: 160; Luckhurst 2005: 11, 124, 243; Seed
2000: 13). As the review in this chapter has demonstrated, the two
genres have followed a largely parallel path to academic respectability
(see also Attebery 1992: 105 and Wolfe 1986, who reach similar conclusions), and they are both centrally concerned with the process of

estrangement and the construction of convincing other worlds. In addition, there is good precedent for continuing to emphasize what unites them rather than what divides them. In a number of places science fiction and fantasy are considered sister genres that naturally fall together as exponents of, for example, the marvellous (Baldick 1990: 129; Brook-Rose 1981), the fantastic (Armitt 1996, 2005; Rose 1981), or the non-mimetic (Clareson 1971; Hume 1984: 123). For Wolfe (2002: 14), they both belong together, along with gothic and horror, in a more or less unified 'set' of texts. For a number of commentators, the generic division between science fiction and fantasy, artificial and imposed to begin with, is unsustainable (Carter 1973: 92; de Camp 1976: 6; Hunt, in Hunt and Lenz 2001/2004: 14; Wolfe 2002: 14). Even Aldiss, who set out to write a definitive history of science fiction, concedes (somewhat grudgingly) to defeat in the attempt to distinguish science fiction from fantasy (Aldiss and Wingrove 1986/2001: 5–6).

It should come as no surprise, then, that some of the same texts have been analysed as science fiction from one perspective, and fantasy from another. Timmerman (1983), for example, treats Herbert's *Dune* as fantasy, even though, as Luckhurst (2005) notes, it is 'still commonly voted the greatest SF novel' (16). Roberts (2006: 31) discusses *Dune* in his study of science fiction, but suggests nevertheless that it has much in common with *The Lord of the Rings* in its depiction of a secondary world. And while *The Lord of the Rings* is typically, indeed emblematically, considered fantasy, it has also been analysed as science fiction (by Meyers 1980, who suggests that its informing science is linguistics). Le Guin's *Earthsea* trilogy, analysed as fantasy by Lenz (in Hunt and Lenz 2001/2004), is treated by Scholes (1975) as science fiction.

Consider as well that one of the traditional dividing lines between science fiction and fantasy, the representation of science in the former and magic in the latter, has been subject to erosion. Aldiss and Wingrove (1986/2001), for example, note that magic remains integral in much 'traditional SF' (229). 'There is', they go on to say, 'a degree of renaming – spells are called "mentally released atomic energy"' (229), but it is magic just the same. For Scholes (1975), one of Le Guin's greatest strengths was her ability to portray magic as though it were science (82). Scholes (1975) also pointed out that the further science fiction projects into the future, the more 'fabulous' (79) the events become, as 'our ability to distinguish the natural from the supernatural diminishes with movement away from present space-time' (70). While Roberts (2006) is careful to distinguish between science fiction and fantasy at the start of his study (6), he nevertheless likens cyberspace in Gibson's *Neuromancer* to 'a near magical realm' in which 'we can soar like the angels' (128), and goes on to observe that 'technology and magic become, as is often the case in SF, only a matter of perspective' (126).

With the generic distinctions under threat generally, and the distance between science fiction and fantasy increasingly closing, it makes sense to consider them as a single conjoined genre. For the purposes of the studies in this book, science fiction and fantasy will be jointly referred to as *alternative world fiction* or *alternative world texts* (unless works I am citing make a clear distinction between them). While other terms for both genres have been suggested and have enjoyed some degree of currency (most notably 'speculative fiction'), *alternative world* captures the primary textual imperative of both, and the focus of the present study: the creation and presentation of plausible and convincing other worlds estranged from the reader's own.

In the present chapter, the development of academic interest in alternative world fiction has been charted from derision to acceptance. It has also been demonstrated that when it comes to the issue of style, however, these texts remain, on the whole, unjustly criticized as pedestrian or inadequate. The first challenge to this judgement begins in the following chapter with an exploration of three alternative world texts that do, contrary to what has previously been claimed, experiment with style for significant thematic reasons.

Chapter 2

Language Contact in
Alternative World Texts:
Experimental Future Englishes

As demonstrated in Chapter 1, discussions of style in alternative world texts have been, in many cases, unfairly dismissive. While it is now widely accepted that these texts cannot be disregarded out of hand as juvenile escapist yarns unworthy of study, ideas about poor or unremarkable style in these narratives seem to persist. Here in this chapter, I deal with one of these remaining ideas, the frequently made claim that alternative world texts tend to avoid experiments in form, sticking instead to more straightforward styles of delivery (see discussion in Chapter 1 of Attebery 2003: 41; Griffin and Wingrove 1984: ix; Irwin 1976; Roberts 2006: 12; Stockwell 2000: 102). To challenge this notion, three texts that clearly do experiment with form, Brian Aldiss's 'A Spot of Konfrontation' (1973, hereafter 'Konfrontation'), Joss Whedon's *Firefly* (2002) and Tad Williams' *Otherland* (1996–2001) are considered. At first glance, these three texts would seem to have little beyond the obvious in common. One is a product of the 1970s ('Konfrontation'); one largely of the 1990s (*Otherland*), and one of the early 2000s (*Firefly*). One is set in space (*Firefly*); one mostly in virtual reality (*Otherland*), and one on Tahiti in the 2070s ('Konfrontation'). *Otherland* is a novel in four volumes that is primarily dark in tone, 'Konfrontation' a short story that is primarily comic, and *Firefly* a television series that is dark with comic elements. Uniting these seemingly disparate alternative world texts, however, is a thematically relevant aspect of style. All of them are futuristic, and all of them propose an English significantly changed by contact with at least one other language as part of that future.

As Lehiste (1988: 28) notes, languages come into contact when speakers of those languages come into contact. When this happens, 'speakers of one language may, deliberately or unconsciously, introduce into their language features of another language to which they have been exposed' (Trask 1999: 151). Contact can lead to many different degrees of change, including lexical borrowing, bilingual phenomena such as code-switching (the regular use of at least two languages in ordinary talk), and even pidginization, the birth of a new language (Crystal 1991: 78; Sebba 1997: 10–14; Trask 1999: 151–2). *Firefly*, *Otherland*, and 'Konfrontation' all use English in an unconventional way, representing varying degrees of contact directly in the language of their narratives in order to suggest changes that may occur in English in the future. In directly representing language contact phenomena as a feature of style, each text explored here demonstrates what is called *affective thematization*. This occurs, as Stockwell (2000: 62) explains, when the language of a story itself is foregrounded, made explicitly noticeable through some difference to or deviance from expectation. As affectively thematized texts, *Firefly*, *Otherland* and 'Konfrontation' make English itself strange. According to Scholes (1975: 47), this kind of linguistic estrangement is typically absent from alternative world fiction. It 'is the new idea that shocks us into perception' (47) and not the language of the text, since this is in most cases, for Scholes (1975: 49), only just about adequate. In the three texts studied in this chapter, however, it is precisely the language of the texts that is made strange, and thus it is the language of the text that 'shocks us into perception'.

In order to explore just what this new perception might be in each case, I draw on and integrate two different approaches to the language of literature, Short's (1989) framework of embedded discourse and Ashcroft et al.'s (1989) articulation of *abrogation* and *appropriation* (37–8). Short (1989) originally devised his framework of embedded discourse with reference to drama dialogue, which, he argued, was 'arranged to be overheard' (149). For Short (1989), characters speaking to each other in drama texts transmit one set of messages. At the same time, however, 'this discourse is part of what the playwright "tells" the audience' (149). This involves two simultaneous channels of communication, one at the character-character level, and one between the text and the audience.[1] The same basic principle has been shown to operate in fictional dialogue (e.g. see Nelson 1991).

Abrogation and *appropriation*, as Ashcroft et al. (1989) explain, are textual strategies often observed at work in post-colonial literatures. Abrogation is a matter of rejecting the status of standard English, while appropriation involves embracing a local variety of English, often markedly different from the standard in form, as the language of the community (Ashcroft et al. 1989: 37–8). A close study of style in *Firefly, Otherland* and 'Konfrontation' suggests that messages about the abrogation of monolingual standard English are being transmitted at the text-audience levels of discourse as characters demonstrate appropriation by using their innovated, estranged future Englishes as already established linguistic norms. While proceeding in this way means that readers and audiences may initially encounter an alienating form of their own language, this same language, as Myers (1983) and Stockwell (2000: 155) note, must also eventually become knowable if the interface between style and theme is to be effective. The discussion of how these opposed aims of linguistic estrangement and understanding are accomplished in each of the three alternative world texts studied here will begin with code-switching in Joss Whedon's *Firefly*.[2]

Code-switching, one of the possible results of language contact, is generally defined as the alternation of two or more languages in the same conversation (Gardner-Chloros et al. 2000: 1306; Gumperz 1982: 59; Myers-Scotton 1993: 1; Wei 2005a: 275). Its representation in other genres, such as Chicano poetry (Fallís 1976; Hedrick 1996; Mendieta-Lombardo and Citron 1995), realist fiction (Gross 2000; Kreml 1998); and drama (Gross 2000) has excited interest, and it is also well-discussed in post-colonial fiction (see Ashcroft et al. 1989). Its potential as a stylistic device in alternative world fiction, however, has been paid only scant attention, perhaps because critical energies have largely gone, as noted in Chapter 1, towards explaining away supposedly poor style rather than focusing on what actually occurs. In the television series *Firefly*, however, the regular use of Chinese-English bilingual code-switching demands attention.

Firefly, as Havens (2003: 132, 134) describes it, is a space western set in the future some 500 years from now, at which time it is supposed that the US and China are the only remaining superpowers. They rule as the totalitarian Anglo-Sino Alliance (*Firefly: The Official Companion, Volume One.* 19). The main characters are a group of former rebels who crew the cargo ship *Serenity*, a so-called Firefly class ship that, while small, is nevertheless a significant annoyance to the larger Alliance vessels it encounters from time to time (*Here's How It Was: The Making of Firefly*, 2003). What do the Chinese-English alternations contribute to this vision of the future? For some commentators, the answer to this question is, 'very little'. Wright (2004), for example, suggests that the Chinese in *Firefly* is simply tokenistic, akin to the chopsticks, Chinese lanterns and pagoda t-shirts that also appear in the show. With reference to the cultural theorist bell hooks, Wright (2004) suggests that the Asian influence in *Firefly*, including what she calls the 'sprinklings of Chinese' (29) in the dialogue, is merely the exotic contained, domesticated and 'made safe' for Western consumption. While tokenism may be a legitimate concern in *Firefly*, I suggest that the representation of Chinese and bilingual code-switching achieves something far more profound. It is through the regular occurrence of Chinese-English code-switching that English is made strange in *Firefly*, and audiences are, through the processes of appropriation and abrogation at work in this estranged future English, prompted to question the current dominance of monolingual standard English.

At the character-character level of discourse in *Firefly*, audiences encounter appropriation as the protagonists instinctively and unproblematically practise code-switching among themselves and with others they meet. We are invited to believe that almost everyone code-switches, 'even the last person you'd expect' (Whedon, quoted in *Here's How It Was: The Making of Firefly*). As the examples below indicate (each from a different episode), we are further invited to believe that for the characters, code-switching is considered ordinary, just a normal part of their talk:

Wash (the pilot):	Well, that's <kwong-juh duh> [nuts], that's suicide; ('Serenity')
Mal (the captain):	Wash, get down to the infirmary <ma-shong> [on the double]; ('Safe')

Kaylee (the mechanic):   But I think it's gonna work. The captain is <jen duh sh tyen tsai> [an absolute genius] when it comes to plans. ('The Train Job')

(The translations, above and throughout this section on *Firefly*, are as given in *Firefly: The Official Companion, Volume One*). In each case, the characters switch from English to Chinese and back again within one conversational utterance. They live in a world where universal Chinese-English bilingualism exists, in terms Myers-Scotton (1993) would use, as a potentially unmarked choice: they experience bilingualism as part of their daily lived existence (1), and the expectation is that they will code-switch with one another. The characters are also represented as code-switching in much the same way as their real-world counterparts would. Drawing on Gumperz (1982), we can say that the characters code-switch

fluently, maintaining an even flow of talk. No hesitation pauses, changes in sentence rhythm, pitch level or intonation contour mark the shift in code. There is nothing . . . to indicate that the speakers don't understand each other. Apart from the alternation itself, the passages have all the earmarks of ordinary conversations in a single language. (Gumperz 1982: 59–60)

They take the presence of Chinese in their society, and their own use of it, entirely for granted. Only once in the whole series (in the episode 'Trash') is the use of Chinese mentioned explicitly, as Sullivan (2004: 198–9) notes, and there are no instances where the use of Chinese presents problems of understanding at the character-character level of discourse. English is in effect refashioned (Ashcroft et al. 1989), its ordinary standard norms re-written, for use in a local community little influenced by what Braj Kachru has called the traditional 'norm-providing' varieties, namely British or American English.

This demonstration of appropriation at the character-character level of discourse in *Firefly* is at the same time a statement of abrogation, a rejection of monolingual standard English as the primary or expected form of communication, at the text-audience level. As the characters regularly and naturally code-switch with each other, audiences are obliged to cope with linguistic behaviour that, from their perspective, is likely to fall outside the norm. While code-switching is ordinary for those who engage in it, and the norm more places in the world than it is not, it is likely to be an unusual occurrence for *Firefly*'s primary audience groups, either monolingual English speakers, or English speakers with little or no knowledge of Chinese. The view of ordinary talk in *Firefly* is not likely to match the audience's view, and this difference may be perceived as exclusion. As Gross (2000) points out in his study of code-switching in drama, purposely switching into a code not known by one's interlocutor can be an aggressive act of rejection, and the code-switched dialogue in *Firefly* takes this stance towards its audience. The Chinese remains untranslated throughout, right down to the subtitles on the DVDs, where the portions of dialogue in Chinese are glossed simply as characters speaking 'the Galactic language'. As Ashcroft et al. (1989) point out, code-switching is by its nature culturally and linguistically syncretic (73–4), and as a stylistic device, it can serve to challenge monocultural and monolingual complacencies (45).

The abrogation/exclusion effect in *Firefly*'s dialogue may be heightened by the presentation of untranslated Chinese as the probable language of greater public presence and prestige. It is shown to be used at all levels of society (from high-ranking Alliance officials to petty thieves), and in a wide range of contexts (at formal parties, during gunfights, for casual chats, in muttered asides). As is typical of majority languages, Chinese in *Firefly* is also the language used for writing, particularly public writing, as Sullivan (2004) points out: we see non-Chinese characters reading Chinese newspapers, and written Chinese in warning notices, shop signs and advertisements (202–5). And, as noted earlier, it is Chinese that is identified as the Galactic language in the show, not English. Consider as well that in multilingual societies, it is usually the prestige language that is used for polite address among strangers (e.g. see LePage and Tabouret-Keller 1985). In *Firefly*, characters switch into Chinese for exactly this purpose. The character Inara, for example, answers a knock on her shuttle door in

Chinese, '<Quing jin> [Come in] ('Serenity'), not English. Similarly, Agent McGinniss, an Alliance official, answers an intercom summons in Chinese with <'Nee hao?'> [Hello?] ('Ariel'). Such usages suggest that Chinese is the higher-status language, not English.

The Chinese-English bilingual code-switching in *Firefly*, along with the presentation of Chinese as the probable majority language, both matters of style, imply a prediction about the possible decline of English as a dominant world language and further signal a possible shift in the balance of power away from the West and towards the Far East. In its incorporation of untranslated Chinese, style in *Firefly* is innovative and far from merely adequate. It is, on the contrary, operational and effective at the most significant level of theme. *Firefly* uses representations of language contact phenomena at the level of style to suggest a more humble future for the English language, and a dramatic change in the global balance of power and influence.[3]

In order for such messages about the demotion of English and Western influence to be transmissible, discernable in the text, the language of that text cannot, as Wright and Hope (1996: 192) point out, be so radically estranged that Anglophone audiences can no longer understand it. This brings us to the second accomplishment of style in *Firefly*. The dialogue in the series presents what is for many members of the audience a foreign and unknown language; at the same time, however, it subtly integrates strategies for the comprehension of that language. Consider, for example, how some of the interactive meanings of code-switching are handled for an audience that is likely to be unfamiliar with them. As studies of real-life code-switching have shown (Brown and Levinson 1978/1987; Gumperz 1982; Myers-Scotton 1992; Williams 2005) one of its communicative functions is to signal intimacy or alignment between interlocutors. This occurs in *Firefly*, as well. In the example below, for instance, Mal, captain and father-figure, switches into Chinese to address Kaylee, mechanic and daughter-figure, with an affectionate endearment.

Mal: Don't go working too hard on that crush <xiao mei mei> [little sister]. Doc won't be with us for long. ('Serenity')

Endearments, as Brown and Levinson (1978/1987) explain, serve to soften potentially face-threatening speech acts, utterances that may be problematic for hearers to receive. In the example above, Mal is producing just such a speech act, a warning to Kaylee not to get too attached to the ship's doctor. This warning may be hard for Kaylee to accept, given her feelings. Mal, who knows this, seeks to ameliorate the effect and stresses his affection for her by issuing the endearment <xiao mei mei> along with the warning. In the context of code-switching between these two characters, the shift into Chinese further underlines the closeness in their relationship. With the key phrase here shifted into Chinese, how is this affective stance communicated to the audience? Such uses of Chinese are scaffolded by employing the same strategy and signalling the same dynamic at times when only English is used, as when Mal says, 'You tell me, now, little Kaylee – you really think you can do this?' ('Bushwhacked').

Thus, in terms of indicating character relationships to the audience, code-switching does not reveal anything that is not also revealed in English. Paralinguistic gestures further serve to denote the father-daughter dynamic between captain and mechanic. Mal often hugs Kaylee in a familiar non-sexual way, and is apt to kiss her on the top of the head. The convergent strategies ensure that an understanding of the relationship between Mal and Kaylee is not dependent on code-switching into Chinese alone.

The surrounding dialogue in *Firefly* supports the use of untranslated Chinese in a number of other ways, as well. Only very rarely, for example, do code-switches into Chinese last for two entire consecutive turns, and there are no instances longer than this. More commonly, switches into Chinese occur within single utterances and involve single words or word-like units. In addition, English is almost exclusively the matrix language, the main language of expression into which the Chinese forms are embedded. This means that most of the dialogue is English in which some Chinese occurs, rather than the other way round. Consider as well that the switched items are often interjections, exclamatives, formulaic responses (Sullivan 2004) or terms of address that are largely predictable in the given contexts. The code-switched elements in the examples below, for instance, participate in common collocations or quasi-formulaic phrases. This makes at least approximate meanings recoverable.

Jayne (hired mercenary):	Why you got us parked here? This ain't the <go tsao de> [dog humping] rendezvous spot; ('The Train Job', 67)
Wash (the pilot):	What the <tyen shiao duh> [name of all that's sacred] is going on here? ('Bushwhacked', 90)
Atherton (villain):	I understand, I'll see you soon, <bao bay> [sweet heart]; ('Shindig', 108)
Older Grange (trader):	They [referring to cattle] ain't well fed. Scrawny.
Mal:	<Fei hua> [nonsense] Hay and milk three times a day. Fed to 'em by beautiful women; (Safe, 130)
Badger (villain):	I place value on the fact that the stick up your <pee-goo> is 'bout as large as the one Harrow's got. ('Shindig', 110)

In the first four examples, where only approximate gisting is possible, it is notable that the Chinese words and phrases are grammatically and semantically non-essential. The final example risks the use of Chinese for a noun that is essential, both in terms of structure and meaning, but that noun, in the phrase given, can really only refer to one thing.

Similar strategies support switches into Chinese that extend across whole utterances. In a number of cases, such utterances are kept short and consist, like the examples above, of single words or word-like units recoverable in context. In the episode 'Safe', Wash is summoned to the infirmary and sees Shepherd Book, gravely, perhaps mortally, injured. Book, a somewhat irreverent preacher, is travelling with the crew and has earned their trust and affection. Coming upon his friend Book in this state, Wash exclaims, '<Lao-tyen, boo>', glossed, predictably, as 'Oh God, no' (136). In another scene, Simon, the ship's doctor, who has just stepped in cow dung, says in frustration '<Niou fun>' (127). Again, the gloss, 'cow poop', is predictable.

Longer switched utterances allow meaning to be recovered in the next turn, in much the same way that it is possible to get the gist of a telephone conversation by listening to only half of it. River, Simon's troubled sister, unhappy about submitting to another round of medical tests, throws some of her brother's medical supplies across the room during an examination. Mal walks by just in time to see this, at which point River says,

> (to Mal) You're not him? (beat) <Liou coe shway duh biao-tze duh ur-tze> [stupid son of a drooling whore and a monkey]. ('Safe', 148)

The next speaking turn is Mal's, and his reaction makes the general nature of River's utterance, if not its exact meaning, clear: 'So she's added cussing and hurling about of things to her repertoire' ('Safe', 148). With some of these longer switched utterances, no reasonable guesses as to linguistic content are supported, but the affective intent is recoverable. Mal, reacting to the news that the Alliance has discovered them, probably due to an onboard spy, says

> <Ni ta ma de. Tianxia suoyoude ren. Dou gaisi> [Everyone under the heavens ought to die]. ('Serenity', 33)

While an approximation of the gloss would be difficult here, it is clear from context that he is making some sort of exclamatory remark born of anxiety and frustration. Similarly, when Kaylee walks away from Mal after he has reprimanded her for not attending to her job, her grumbled exit line '<Kuh-oo duh lao bao jurn>', is clearly some sort of complaint about him ('Horrible old tyrant', as it turns out) ('The Train Job', 58).

While integrated comprehension strategies like these may have led commentators such as Wright (2004) to conclude that the Chinese in *Firefly* is superficial, a fairer evaluation takes into account what Myers (1983) reminds us must happen when it is the language of the text itself that serves as the estranged element in alternative world fiction. *Firefly* challenges audiences with a future English sufficiently different from their own, but ensures eventual understanding of the code through non-intrusive devices that still allow messages about the de-privileging of monolingual standard English to be communicated at audience-text level. Audiences are presented with a rejection of their own language in terms they can nevertheless come to understand.

The second text for consideration here, Tad Williams' *Otherland*, meets a very similar textual challenge in a similar range of ways. Described by Williams (1998/1999) himself in an Author's Note as a 'very, very long novel', *Otherland* is set in the mid-twenty-first century and consists of four volumes, *City of Golden Shadow* (1996/1998, cited here as V1), *River of Blue Fire* (1998/1999, cited here as V2), *Mountain of Black Glass* (1999/2000, cited here as V3), and *Sea of Silver Light* (2001/2002, cited here as V4). In the novel, the world-wide-web has become a network of virtual reality (VR) simulations that users can plug into via a neural link. The central conflict, spanning all four volumes, revolves around a group of obscenely wealthy, powerful and extremely aged individuals who have joined forces as the Grail Brotherhood to exploit the VR technology in order to find a way to permanently divorce consciousness from the body. Their ultimate goal is to live forever online and, given the properties of cyberspace suggested in the novel, all powerfully as pure thought in the VR net-work. They are frustrated in their attempts by a group of characters drawn together to oppose them when they realize that either they themselves or their loved ones are trapped in the VR network by the activities of the Brotherhood. While they battle against the Brother-hood from inside the network, their physical bodies either languish in comas, or are sustained artificially in specially designed tanks.

The comparisons with Gibson's *Neuromancer* are obvious and have been made. Conn (2001), for example, puts *Otherland* beside Gibson's work and looks at how both of them extrapolate the possibilities of VR technology to explore 'what it means to be human or even posthuman' (217). For Conn (2001), *Otherland* offers various rich avenues of interpretation. It invites us to ponder 'what is real and what is not' (Conn 2001: 216); to contemplate 'new ways and places for con-sciousness to exist' (214); and to consider how the characters trapped in VR worlds created by others 'become human viruses, corrupting plot patterns that have remained intact since *The Iliad* and *The Odyssey*' (216). Themes of equal salience, however, emerge from a study of style in *Otherland*, an issue that does not interest Conn (2001).

The futuristic VR setting of Williams' novel is not simply a matter of extrapolated technology. Williams also extrapolates a possible future variety of English, 'net-slang', that has, it is suggested, developed alongside (perhaps more appropriately 'inside') the technology.[4] While English is rhetorically identified in the novel as 'the common language in most international VR environments' (V1: 503), its net-slang variety appears to be the language of actual usage, at least among the teenagers and younger users who are equally at home online as well as off. In part, net-slang is characterized by the metaphoric use of terms from the computing industry, such as *scan* and *systems*. *Systems* appears to mean something like 'operating normally' or 'okay' ('Are you gonna be systems for tomorrow?', V2: 45), and *scan* (also *scanned, scanny, scanning* and *scanbark*) seems to be an adjective applied to things and events that are anything from just sort of weird to highly disturbing ('Something's gone utterly, utterly scanned with the whole thing', V2: 107).

Even more interesting in net-slang, however, is the evidence of contact. Like the code-switched dialogue in *Firefly*, net-slang in *Otherland* is presented as influenced by contact, and, I suggest, for a similar purpose: forecasting a shift of global power away from the Anglo-American centre. The use of net-slang in *Otherland*, like the use of Chinese-English alternations in *Firefly*, simultaneously dramatizes the process of appropriation, the shared and accepted use of a non-standard English, at the character-character level of discourse, and abrogation, the de-privileging of standard English, at the text-reader level.

A noticeable feature of net-slang for many Anglophone readers at the text-reader level of discourse in *Otherland* will be the incorporation of what is, or is meant to look like, Chinese or Japanese lexis that is treated as normal at the character-character level[5]:

Chinese:
We supposed to sniff for some *sayee lo* net-knocker? (V1: 903)
Don't want no more *sayee lo* fish-swallowing, me; (V2: 159)
That is so *tchi seen*; (V2: 249)
Tchi seen, Orlando, you really think so? God! (V2: 357)

We've got some weird stuff going on – *tchi seen* major sampled; (V1: 218)[6]

. . . a picture of this *ho ying* guy with a sword; (V1: 521)

You shouldn't be listening to that *fen*; (V2: 592)

Ho dzang! said Fredericks; (V2: 154)

Dzang, yeah. I can work a boat; (V2: 159)

Dzang, man. *Ho dzang*. Utterly chizz.[7] That was one of your best ever; (V1: 363)

. . . just float like some *sayee lo* butterfly. (V4: 1129)

Japanese:

Ichiban! Got it! (V1: 642)

We got chased out of TreeHouse by a bunch of old *akisushi*. (V1: 683)

Net-slang also distinguishes itself from standard English through marked uses of reduplication in which entire words are repeated:

Oh, *fenfen*, Fredericks, use your brain; (V1: 359)

Fenfen, I'm sick of water; (V2: 599)

Then wet wet splash splash; (V3: 27)

Come *now fast-fast-fast*. (V1: 770)

While reduplication occurs in standard English, it tends, as Thun (1963) notes, to be of a different type. Instead of repeating identical lexical units to indicate emphasis or iteration, as above, reduplication in standard English generally involves sound-units (e.g. *shilly-shally*) (Thun 1963). When identical reduplication does occur, it is often restricted to playful or conversational language (e.g. representing sounds, nursery rhymes and words, interjections and informal derogatory exaggerations) (Thun 1963: 210–11). The reduplicated items represented in *Otherland* are not restricted in this way; rather, they are used as part of the 'ordinary' word-stock in net-slang. In addition, the use of reduplication in net-slang can generate meanings other than emphasis or iteration. When one of the net-slang users asks if someone is a 'funny-funny man' (V1: 672), he is not asking if the man is very funny, but if he is a pervert of some kind. The incorporation of a relatively un-English type of reduplication, like the use of Chinese and Japanese lexis, suggests that contact with other languages is an important feature of net-slang.

For the net-slang users in *Otherland*, such influences are the norm. Intensifying this represented appropriation are various indications that net-slang is not some superficial here-today-and-gone-tomorrow linguistic fad, but a variety that is beginning to establish itself. Its use of reduplication, for example, indicates that it has lasted long enough to incorporate a grammatical pattern. As Aitchison (1991) notes, lexical items are among the first elements to transfer from one lan- guage or variety to another, while grammatical changes tend to take longer. Their incorporation suggests a more sustained and regular period of contact. Notice as well that reduplication in net-slang is represented as productive. Its use is not confined to borrowed lexis such as *fen*, but is used with ordinary English words like *wet, splash* and *funny*. While the characters who use net-slang often seem to consider it an in-group code, there are signs that its use has spread to other contexts, as well. It occurs not only in the speech of many of the young protagonists, but also in their literature. The character Irene, for example, while reading a detective story to her younger brother (trapped in a coma induced by the activities of the Grail Brotherhood), encounters net-slang in the dialogue ('That's some viscious-bad wonton!' V1: 110). Many characters, whether they use net-slang or not, or approve of it or not, are shown to be explicitly aware of it, calling it, variously, 'net-girl slang' (V1: 514) or 'Junior Netboy argot' (V1: 34–5) or 'goggle-boy' (V1: 901) (see note 4). In addition, its speakers recognize poor or inappropriate usage. One young user, for example, is unimpressed when a computer company executive uses net-slang in an effort to recruit him. For him, her use of the code is artificial and forced: she speaks it as 'someone who knew she would not be able to get away with using net-girl slang much longer' (V1: 514).

Net-slang, represented as an appropriating contact variety that looks beyond mother-tongue English for its developing norms,[8] indicates a shift away from an assumed Anglo-American perspective in more subtle ways, as well. Consider, for example, the net-slang noun phrase *this ho-ying guy with a sword* (V1: 521). Orlando, the character speaking here, is not Asian or of Asian descent, and he lives with his parents in one of America's 'exclusive communities' (V1: 373). It is as a speaker of net-slang that he uses this phrase in partial explanation of how he developed his VR persona in a fantasy role-playing game. The game is set in a pseudo-medieval world called 'Middle Country' (V1: 102), clearly a thinly veiled reference to Tolkien's Middle Earth in *The Lord of the Rings*. Orlando's character is a barbarian warrior, the idea for which he got from a picture on the cover of an old book.

> This kid I used to go to school with, his father had all these old books – y'know, paper. One had a picture on the cover of this *ho ying* guy with a sword. It was called 'Thangor' or something like that. I just changed it a little bit when I first started out in the Middle Country. (V1: 521)

The barbarian warrior named something like 'Thangor' closely echoes Lin Carter's creation, the barbarian warrior Thongor (in, for example, *The Wizard of Lemuria*, 1965), and Carter (1973), like a number of sword and sorcery writers, as he himself notes, is happily indebted to Robert E. Howard and his creation Conan, 'that prototype of all sword and sorcery heroes' (Carter 1973: 63). In Orlando's net-slang, a barbarian warrior in the tradition of Conan, a significant element of Anglo-American popular culture, is described from an Asian point of reference. While 'Middle Country' and 'Thangor' may be knowing intertextual homages, they are also spontaneously recoded in the dialogue as part of an Asian cultural heritage by an American youngster's automatic use of *ho ying*.

The naming strategies in *Otherland* also suggest contact, and reinforce the shifted perspective evident in the use of net-slang. As Taylor (1990: 613) has suggested, the use of WASP-y (white, Anglo-Saxon Protestant) or Scottish-descent names (e.g. Cliff McClane, Brad Johnson, etc.) for heroes and protagonists often goes hand-in-hand with an uncontested Anglo-American outlook. In contrast, *Otherland* presents as the norm a host of distinctly un-WASP-y names, such *Olga Pirofsky, Jiun Bhao, Hideki Kunohara* and *Del Ray Chiume*. Such names apply to major characters (*Irene Sulaweyo, !Xabbu, Orlando Gardiner,*

Felix Jongleur); minor ones (*Calliope Skouros, Bolivar Atasco*); and those that appear only briefly (*Tillamook Taillard Jensen, Hussein Mbinda, Murat Sagar Singh* and *Gwa Choi* – a superintendent of schools in Arkansas).

Place names work in a similar way. The characters trapped in VR are all haunted by visions of a seemingly mythical golden city, descriptions of which reveal an Asian frame of reference rather than an Anglo-American one. It is compared not to Chicago or New York or London, but to major cities in China and Japan: 'a metropolis with elaborately decorated buildings as tall as anything in Hong Kong or Tokyokahama' (V1: 25) (this last perhaps an indication that Tokyo and Okahama have merged into a single conurbation). The same effect is achieved when the character Irene describes the vastness of the VR network with reference to a major Chinese city: 'If you tried to visit every node on the net, or even just every node in this Mall . . . well, it would be like trying to call every single address in the Greater Beijing Directory' (V1: 67). Names of firms, products and places of business reflect the same shifted perspective, whether seemingly casual, such as the 'Krittapong Home Entertainment Unit' (V1: 70), or more explicitly central. The sign for the virtual nightclub Mister J's, for example, a front for the Grail Brotherhood, is written, as one character notes, not just in English, but also in 'Japanese, Chinese, Arabic, and a few other alphabets' (V1: 50).

The contact phenomena in *Otherland* is, in Le Guin's terms, more than just icing on the cake (see earlier discussion on page 15). Written and published with the English-speaking Anglo-American market in mind, *Otherland* nevertheless uses style to abrogate the language of its own context at the text-reader level through the representation of appropriated contact phenomena at the character-character level. In confronting readers with an estranged form of their own language, *Otherland* presents an assumed milieu shifted away from their perspective. Like the code-switched utterances in *Firefly*, the contact phenomena in *Otherland* encode a matter of theme, challenging Anglo-American cultural and linguistic supremacy at the level of style.

Estrangement embedded at the level of style can only be effective, of course, if the estranged code carries with it the key to its eventual understanding. Towards this end, net-slang is used in such a way that this initially alienating code subtly integrates support mechanisms for its eventual decoding. The actual number of borrowed elements is kept small, for instance, and they manifest mostly at the lexical level, with foreign terms inserted into what is otherwise an English clause. This allows knowledge of English syntactic structure, available intuitively if not explicitly through a reader's linguistic competence, to serve as a partial guide to meaning (see also Stockwell 2000: Chapter 7). If we look more closely at phrases such as 'so *tchi seen*' we can, for example, work out from the use of *so* that *tchi seen* must be an adjective of some kind in this case, since adjectives in English can themselves be premodified with intensifying adverbials like *so*. In a similar way, *fen*, *fenfen* and *akisushi* in the phrases 'that *fen*', 'utter *fenfen*' and 'a bunch of old *akisushi*' can be identified as nouns because they all behave like nouns in English: *fen* follows the demonstrative determiner *that*; *fenfen* is modified by the intensifying attributive adjective *utter*; and *akisushi* is premodified by the central adjective *old*. Knowledge of English noun phrase structure also tells us that *sayee lo* (in '*sayee lo* net-knocker', '*sayee lo* fish-swallowing', and '*sayee lo* butterfly') can be classified as an adjective or an item serving as an adjective, since it premodifies head nouns such as *net-knocker* (someone who wanders at random through VR simulations), *fish-swallowing* and *butterfly*.

The partial disambiguations made possible by syntactic structure are supported by two further stylistic mechanisms, co-textual translations and repeated usage. These allow for more refined guesses to be made as to what the borrowed terms might mean. Consider, for instance, the following piece of dialogue (parts of which have been instanced earlier) from the character who calls himself T4b online, and whose VR persona is a transformer-type robot.

We supposed to sniff for some *sayee lo* net-knocker? [. . .] While someone trying to six us? You *far* far crash! (V1: 903, ellipses mine)

The wider co-text (surrounding language) of this phrase is this:

Sellars took a ragged breath; his shapeless form seemed to sag. 'There is a man named Jonas. He was a prisoner of The Grail Brotherhood, his mind held captive in a simulation. I was able to reach him when he dreamed. I helped him escape. Look for him.'

'We supposed to sniff for some *sayee lo* net-knocker?' The battle-robot waved its arms, flashing the razor-sharp blades at its joints. 'While someone trying to six us? You *far* far crash!' (V1: 903)

Here, Sellars, a character who speaks standard English, makes a suggestion, to which T4b reacts with incredulity by repeating it in his own variety, net-slang. Repetitions for the purpose of expressing disbelief occur naturally in English conversation, and it is also natural in the fictional world of *Otherland* that T4b should respond in his own variety. At the same time, however, this naturalistic exchange embeds a standard English translation of T4b's net-slang. Such translations supplement the structural information and allow for more precise meanings of the contact-influenced loan words and phrases to be inferred. The 'net-knocker', we now know, is the character Jonas, whose mind is imprisoned in the VR network. The structural clues and the standard English translation of T4b's utterance lead up to a probable gloss of 'crazy' or 'unlucky' for *sayee lo*. This gloss can be tested against the repeated occurrences of *sayee lo* in other contexts. In one of the other VR worlds, T4b has the disturbing experience of being swallowed by a fish, the context for '*saylee lo* fish-swallowing'. It is T4b who also notices a strange creature that appears to float and drift its way through the simulated worlds, hence '*sayee lo* butterfly'. In both of these repeated uses, the probable meaning of 'crazy' or 'unlucky' for *saylee lo* is reinforced. In a posting on the message board of the official Tad Williams website (http://www.tadwilliams.com), the author confirms that *sayee lo* is intended to mean either 'crazy' or 'stupid' (post registered on 30 May 2001).

Through the use of embedded translations and repeated occurrences in the same structural environments, the initially alienating contact phenomena in net-slang gradually become more comprehensible. A probable meaning for *fenfen*, for example, builds up gradually over repeated uses in the dialogue:

Oh, *fenfen*, Fredericks, use your brain; (V1: 359)
That's *fenfen*. You always get your way Orlando, and I always pay for it; (V1: 490)
That's utter *fenfen* Gardiner; (V1: 513)

. . . you got me into this impacted, *fenfen* mess in the first place;
    (V1: 839)
Fenfen. I don't believe you; (V2: 176)
Oh, *fenfen*; (V2: 231)
Fenfen, I'm sick of water. (V2: 599)

As more and more uses of *fenfen* are encountered, it becomes clear
both from syntactic placement and context of use that it is some sort
of exclamative expletive that can occur variously not only as a noun
but also as an adjective, perhaps akin to English terms such as *crap*
and *crappy*. This is plausible as the term *fen* means *manure* (according
to Chen 1970, *A Practical English-Chinese Pronouncing Dictionary*).

By introducing contact phenomena at the lexical level, opportunities
for working out at least probable meanings for the estranged items
are maintained. Uses of net-slang extending beyond the lexical
level are similarly sensitive. Reduplication mostly affects adverb and
adjective phrases, leaving the basic English clause structure intact.
Net-slang also makes effective use of non-standard dialect variation
to suggest the speech of 'fluent' speakers. Instead of increasing the
use of loan words, or radically disrupting the syntax of the clause,
non-standard forms of English are used alongside the contact phenomena to suggest both greater distance from standard English
and net-slang fluency. This allows for both alienation and comprehension, as can be demonstrated by another look at T4b's dialogue.
Of all the net-slang users, T4b is identified, both through narratorial
assessment and his own speech, as the most 'fluent' (V1: 902)
speaker:

Just want out this far crash place, me; (V2: 33)
Feel pure *fen fen* me. Fish ate me . . . puked me up, too . . . Doing
    that again? Never; (V2: 63)
Saying this some tabnet-like conspiracy? . . . Space aliens, something?
    Far scanning, you; (V1: 860)
You wanna know my ID for what? You with netnews? (V2: 156)
Ain't telling no names; (V2: 156)
Here for my shadow, me; (V2: 156)
Saw some kind of animal, us. (V3: 36)

As the examples above indicate, T4b's fluency is indicated not by increasing the representation of contact phenomena or disturbing English clause patterns, but by manipulating the English elements of his code. Fairly consistent features include the omission of subject pronouns ('[*I*] just want out'; '[*I*] feel pure *fen fen*'; '[*it*] puked me up'; [*We*] saw some kind of animal), the omission of both the subject pronoun and auxiliary *to be* ('[*Are you*] saying this'; '[*Am I*] doing that again'; [*I am*] here for my shadow), the omission of *to be* as a main verb ('this [*is*] some tabnet-like conspiracy?'), and the omission of articles ('[*A*] fish ate me'). Also interesting in T4b's language is his use of object pronouns. While subject pronouns are often omitted, the subject material often appears as a clause-final element in an object pronoun ('Just want out this far crash place, *me*'; 'Feel pure *fen fen me*'; 'Far scanning *you*'; 'Saw some kind of animal, *us*'; 'Here for my shadow, *me*'). Such elements suggest a far greater level of divergence than loan words alone while still allowing a reasonable degree of comprehension for Anglophone readers.

Other elements of the narrative scaffold the estranged English by carrying a convergent thematic message. All of the chapters, for example, begin with broadcasts from NETFEED, the online equivalent of a major daily newspaper. Many of these bear no obvious relation to the plot, but what they do show reinforces the messages suggested by the contact-influenced dialogue and naming strategies: a shift in the global balance of power. Many of the NETFEED broadcasts reflect, in the guise of background information that is only casually encountered, an America in decay. Readers find out through NETFEED, for example, that acts of domestic terrorism are claimed as performance art (V2: 450), and that adult children sue their parents for not being sufficiently politically correct while they were growing up, thus leaving them handicapped in adulthood with 'racial intolerance, health-issues insensitivity', etc. (V2: 534). Arkansas schoolchildren have to wear safety helmets at school all day unless their parents sign an indemnity form (V2: 25). Political lobbying has become completely institutionalized with the establishment of an Industrial Senate (V2: 394), and there are calls to have religious groups represented in the same way (V2: 420). The NETFEEF broadcasts also reveal that extreme poverty has created a generation of street children, and that the police response to this situation is to accept bribes from shops and retailers to have

them 'removed' (i.e. killed) (V2: 470). Such broadcasts show an erosion of traditional societal institutions: the government, the law, the
criminal justice system, universal education. With America in such
decline, power and influence have shifted away from the West and
towards the Far East. As one NETFEED broadcast puts it, 'the future
belongs to a United Asia' (V1: 65), so much so, according to *Otherland*,
that a new variety of English, heavily influenced by contact with Asian
languages, has developed and is taking hold, and readers encounter
the new variety directly in the language of the text itself. As in *Firefly*,
an innovative and experimental style in *Otherland* carries theme.

The third and final text to be explored here is Brian Aldiss's short
story 'A Spot of Konfrontation'. 'Konfrontation' is set in the early
2070s, when the citizens of first-world European 'Market States'
are obliged to holiday in the Third World in order to keep the 'Global
Trade Balance' stable (96) (this and all subsequent references to
'Konfrontation' are from the 1983 reprint in *New Arrivals, Old
Encounters*). They are given a set travel allowance in order to do this,
and the protagonist of the story, Gunpat Smith, is on such a holiday
in Tahiti with his family. It all goes wrong when he has an affair
with a prostitute named Flavia and finds himself stranded as a
'displaced tourist' (91) when his wife uses the remaining travel miles
to fly home without him.

The speech of Gunpat, Flavia, and several of the other characters
in 'Konfrontation' is affectively thematized, deliberately made
noticeable, as the following examples demonstrate:

Is es total doomwatch? (89)
Vous geht zuruck to UK to-dago, by la mambo-jet? (81)
Phew, dies temperturo! (78)
Jeg kenna die rialto perfecto hide-out! (90)
Die kommodities restera fail-safe in Hans' villa; (90)
Die Politzie mussa be on mine number; (88)
Flavia, jeg mussa speech mit vous; (88)
Oh, jeg mucho amora. Rialto wunderbar; (82)
I'm okay, danke. And vous, Rosie? Cheers! (81)

This is very clearly English made strange. As was the case in *Firefly* and
Otherland, this strangeness comes about through the representation

of contact phenomena. Of the 55 words that comprise these examples, only about a third are actually English, and most of those are prepositions, pronouns, forms of the verb *to be* and interjections (*Phew, Oh*). With only few exceptions (e.g. *doomwatch, -jet*), the semantic content words appear to be drawn not from English but from Norwegian, German, French, Spanish and Italian.

Just what is this created language in 'Konfrontation' and why has it been proposed? To tackle the first question first, it can be argued that the created language of 'Konfrontation' is represented as a pidgin. Pidgin languages, as Sebba (1997) explains, develop when groups of people who have no common language, and little incentive to learn each other's languages, have to communicate regularly over long periods of time. As they do so, a new language, the pidgin, comes into being (Sebba 1997; Todd 1974/1990). While the typical examples of pidgin languages given are those arising out of the slave trade and imperial conquest, they can also arise in more mundane circumstances, such as tourism (Sebba 1997). It is clear in 'Konfrontation' that the circumstances under which pidgins develop, particularly tourist pidgins, obtain. The first-world Europeans who take their obliged holidays have no incentive to learn each other's languages, or the local language, as they are just vacationing. The tourism directive, however, brings the same language groups together in the same place often enough, and for long enough, that sustained communication becomes necessary. Pidgins are also largely an adult language-learning phenomenon and are thus no-one's native language (Todd 1974/1990: 4), and this too appears as a represented feature of the created language of 'Konfrontation'. Characters with differing native languages (Gunpat speaks English, Flavia Italian, and there are references to German, French and Japanese as well), have, it is suggested in 'Konfrontation', picked up the created language as adults out of communicative necessity.

Structural suggestions of pidginization are also there to be found in the created language of 'Konfrontation'.[9] As in many actual English-based pidgins, the verb *to be* is often omitted in equational sentences:

UK lange wego from Tahiti (76) / The UK *is* a long way from Tahiti;
Jeg high-rise to be here (77) / I *am* happy to be here;

and there is an invariant negator:

> Englisch nix speec! (84) / Don't speak English!
> Nix somna? (82) / You didn't sleep?
> Politzei nix find (84) / The police won't find it.

Pidgin languages tend to draw their vocabulary items from the higher status language in the contact situation, but these vocabularies tend, at least at first, to be limited. This means that one word in the pidgin may cover a larger range of meanings than it did in the source language. 'Konfrontation' shows evidence of this process in the use of *ven*, which seems to mean *if, when* and *whether.*

> Ven vous reviendra to Papeete nexta jahr (82) / When you return
>   to Papeete next year
> Ven jeg sensera alto or elle sensera low (88) / Whether I feel high
>   or she feels low
> Ven jeg fortunato! (81) / If I am lucky

The omission of *to be*, invariant negation, and multi-functional lexical items reflect the early stages of pidginization, when material from the source languages is used but simplified to meet the demands of adult language learners in the on-the-spot, face-to-face communication that characterizes pidgin development (Sebba 1997; Todd 1974/1990). As Sebba (1997) notes, however, pidgins that continue to play an important role for their speakers tend to persist over time and undergo further development. The pidgin in 'Konfrontation' appears to have made it to this stage. There is, for example, evidence for development in its inflectional morphology, a key indicator of increasing complexity in a developing pidgin (Sebba 1997). It appears that the verb for 'sleep' in the created language in 'Konfrontation' has at least two forms, the imperative *somn-a* (as in 'sleep well', 80), and a non-finite *somn-o* ('it is too hot to sleep/for sleeping', 80). In addition, two future tenses are suggested in inflections adapted from French, *–iendra* (*reviendra* [82], will/going to return) and *–era* (*restera* [81], stay; *amorera* [82], like; *findera* [82], find; *sensera* [88], feel). The rudiments of a personal pronoun system are also indicated (e.g. *jeg* for I; *vous* for you; *elle* for she), as well as a demonstrative (*dies* in *dies rummet*, 80) and a consistent definite article (*die* in *die schip* and *die rialto perfect hide-out*, 84).

As pidgins develop, they also tend to be used for a greater number of functions and in more complex situations and can become important lingua francas for the communities and societies in which they are spoken (Todd 1974/1990: 5). The pidgin in 'Konfrontation' bears just such hallmarks of development. It is the language of everyday communication in a multilingual society whose members have no other common language. It is used in writing (80), sung in pop songs (88), and is so well established, in fact, that some of its lexical items have found their way into the standard English spoken at the British Consulate ('it would make me terribly high-rise to be able to sort things out', 84). The created language in 'Konfrontation' is even used when characters talk to themselves, as when Gunpat rhetorically addresses the absent Flavia ('You'd rialto better be back by middago my girl', 76).

Developing pidgins also tend to become more stylistically complex and enrich their range of conceptual reference over time (Sebba 1997: 106, 117). One of the ways they do this is through metaphorical extension, whereby words for familiar things come to take on metaphorical meanings (Sebba 1997: 119). This is how 'high-rise', familiar as a type of building in 'Konfrontation', seems to have developed the sense of *happy* or *delighted* in the created pidgin, as evident in the examples briefly cited earlier: *Jeg high-rise to be here* (77); *it would make me terribly high-rise to be able to sort things out* (84). Pidgins also tend to adopt informal conversational lexis from their source languages as 'standard' terms (Sebba 1997), and this feature would seem to account for the use of 'waz-wot': *Abe kenna waz-wot in Papeete* (88) / *Abe knows what's what in Papeete*; 'overkill' (*It's overkill possible*, 86; *I am relying on you overkill!*, 83); and 'bang-bang' (*Nix bang-bang!*, 95).

As Sebba (1997) observes, another clear indication that a pidgin is becoming increasingly established is the development of fixed norms of use. As structures develop, they become conventionalized, and speakers have very clear ideas about 'what is and what is not a word of the pidgin' (Sebba 1997: 116), what is or is not an acceptable structure and what is or is not an appropriate pronunciation (Sebba 1997: 105, 116). The speakers of the language in 'Konfrontation' exhibit just this sort of normative stance, and it is clear that they consider it to *be* a language. There are, for example, several references to characters who speak the language badly in a 'broken' (76) or 'stumbling' (84) form, and there are also characters who find themselves unable to remember the word for a particular item (83).

While Konfrontation's created pidgin is fictional and thus could not stand as an actual pidgin, it nevertheless represents many of the key indicators of a pidgin at an advanced stage of development: growing syntactic complexity, metaphorical extension, diverse range of use, and the development of fixed norms. In representing this pidgin, 'Konfrontation' clearly demonstrates an experiment with form, making the language of the text itself strange. What purpose does this estrangement serve? The critical literature is not much help here. While it is no surprise that Aldiss, one of the prime exemplars of new wave sf (see earlier discussion on page 17), has produced a stylistically experimental piece of work, the experiment in 'Konfrontation' does not seem to have attracted much attention, despite a reprint of the story in Aldiss's collection *New Arrivals, Old Encounters* (1979). Apart from citation entries in lists of Aldiss's work and popular reviews, such as *Thomas Disch's Science Fiction Picks* (2007), the story is hardly mentioned, and even studies dedicated to Aldiss and his work pay it scant attention (see, for example, Henighan 1999; Mathews 1977; McNelly 1982; Wingrove 1979). Mathews (1977), for instance, bills his work as one of the first major studies of Aldiss, and highlights Aldiss's concerns with language and stylistic technique. 'Konfrontation', however, is not discussed. Wingrove (1979), in an article on then-recent work from Aldiss, does not mention 'Konfrontation' either.

It might be tempting to deal with 'Konfrontation' in the same way that David Ketterer (1974: 260), as noted in Chapter 1 (see pages 17–18), dealt with *Barefoot in the Head*. That is, it might be dismissed as a stylistic experiment gone out of control, an indulgent focus on form that has lost sight of meaning to its cost. Careful analysis, however, reveals that the represented pidgin in 'Konfrontation' is not simply textual play for its own sake, but integral to the issue of theme. 'Konfrontation' can be read as a satire of Europe's relationship with the third world. As Mathews (1977: 14) has noted, Aldiss is a gifted satirist and one of his most frequently visited themes is the 'welfare state's relation with its public and foreign nationals'. In one brief note on 'Konfrontation' in their book-length study of Aldiss's work, Griffin and Wingrove (1984: 241, n.107) place the story as one among many of Aldiss's depictions of Western civilization and the third world 'at war with each other and yet dependent upon each other economically.' The name of the created language in 'Konfrontation' is spEEC, which clearly recalls the European Economic Community. When the EEC was first formed in 1957, it united, as Lister (1988) notes, not only the first six member states (Germany, France, Belgium, Italy, Luxembourg and the Netherlands), but also their dependencies in the third world. As Lister (1988: xii) goes on to point out, trade preferences were established and financial aid was made available, but the relationship, which she refers to as 'welfare neocolonialism' (13), remained unequal. Initiatives were later put in place through the European Regional Development Fund to enable richer nations to support poorer ones through investment, job creation and improved infrastructure (http://europarl.org.uk), but colonial echoes remained and the rhetorical commitments to 'equal partnerships' were never fully realized (Lister 1988; Stevens 1984). 'Konfrontation', with its richer 'market state' citizens obliged to support their poorer third world cousins through obligatory holidays in an arrangement that benefits no one, can be read as a comic but nevertheless scathing commentary on this state of affairs.

With this thematic backdrop in place, spEEC might be thought of as a kind of Euro-babble offered to mirror the absurdity of the situation depicted, or some sort of statement on English's inevitable decline, a theme common enough, as Meyers (1980: 36) notes, in science fiction. However, it is difficult to sustain either the spEEC-as-babble thesis, or the spEEC-as-English-in-decline thesis, since spEEC is clearly not presented as gibberish. Rather, it is depicted, as the preceding analysis has just demonstrated, as an effective and functioning lingua franca that is reasonably well-established in the community. It might be supposed that *this* is the point of spEEC. While pidgins are popularly devalued as 'inferior, haphazard, broken, bastardized versions of older, longer established languages' (Todd 1974/1990: 1), linguistic study has revealed that they are legitimate and rule-governed systems of linguistic communication (Sebba 1997), and spEEC could be interpreted as representing this view. To assume that spEEC simply actualizes a given scholarly view on pidgin languages, however, seems to impose a linguistic reading rather than apply one.

What, then, might be the significance of spEEC in 'Konfrontation'? I suggest here that spEEC, like net-slang in *Otherland* and Chinese-English bilingualism in *Firefly*, represents appropriation and abrogation in progress as a feature of style in order to indict first-world arrogance as a matter of theme. As Sebba (1997: 123) notes, if a pidgin lasts and becomes sufficiently important to its users, it evolves in an increasingly independent direction: it 'has its own mind' (123) and is 'the master of its own resources' (123). The process of pidginization as described by linguists such as Sebba (1997) can be taken as an instance of Ashcroft et al.'s (1989) process of appropriation. This appropriation is carried through to the character-character level of discourse. While Gunpat maintains a sneering attitude towards spEEC (85), he does accept it as a necessary part of his daily life, as do most of the other characters. As they converse in spEEC, a time-lapse view of appropriation unfolds before our eyes in vivid linguistic detail. Words and structures from the source languages are adopted, but then significantly re-made to suit a new community of users: familiar words become new metaphors, colloquial phrases set new standards, shuffled inflections give rise to new verb paradigms.

At the text-audience level of discourse, the representation of spEEC plays an abrogating role by presenting English and various other major languages of first-world Europe not as imposed languages of prestige, but as increasingly irrelevant lexifiers (suppliers of vocabulary) in a thriving pidgin. In 'Konfrontation', a first-world tourism policy rooted in unthinking arrogance is shown to backfire. What may have been intended as a means to prosperity for all creates instead a population of displaced tourists whose only means of income is crime. Gunpat, for example, unwillingly falls in with a smuggling ring as it is the only way he can support himself as a displaced tourist barred from legitimate employment. As the story progresses, it becomes clear that some of the other characters are in the same position as Gunpat. He discovers to his surprise, for example, that Flavia is not a native girl as he first thought, but a displaced tourist like himself. Abandoned by her husband on a holiday trip, she was forced into prostitution to survive. The other members of Gunpat's smuggling ring may have suffered similar fates. While Gunpat is struggling to return home, Flavia and the others appear to have given up on that long ago, and have made what life they can as the permanently displaced. The last laugh, in this satirical piece, however, may be theirs. While any reading suggesting the development of a cohesive community organized to resist hegemonic interference would be difficult to advance,[10] the displaced tourist population is finding its own means of sustenance as it becomes increasingly severed from its original first-world communities and governments. As it develops along its own lines, its lingua franca becomes increasingly independent from its first-world source languages, which are not just abrogated but fully absorbed into the developing pidgin they speak. Style in 'Konfrontation', clearly not pedestrian and much more than simply adequate, realizes a central element of theme by estranging the language of its own telling.

Like the code-switched dialogue in *Firefly* and the net-slang in *Otherworld*, spEEC in 'Konfrontation' has to be sufficiently different from the language of the story's readership, but at the same time ultimately knowable (Myers 1983). In another coup for style in 'Konfrontation', spEEC meets this condition: the created pidgin is initially alienating, but designed at the same time to be decipherable. Our first extended experience with spEEC comes early in the story in the form of a note that Flavia leaves for Gunpat.

> 'Helo Gunny! Jeg exita. Apologia fur absenso. Too much temperturo in dies rummet fur somno, als eterno. Jeg reviendra par middago. Somna vohl! Amor, Flavia'. (75)

The note, worked seamlessly into the plot, also serves to train the reader to cope with the estranged text. To start with the more straight-forward elements of the analysis, the note has an obvious and easily decodable opening and closing: *Helo Guny* and *Amor, Flavia* are clearly 'Hello Gunny' and 'Love, Flavia.' *Fur* occurs twice, both times in positions and contexts that suggest the English preposition 'for' (*fur somno* and *fur absenso*), allowing initial guesses regarding its meaning to be confirmed. Many of the other vocabulary items here closely resemble existing English words with Latinate derivations:

exita	exit
apologia	apology
absenso	absence
temperturo	temperature
eterno	eternal

Somno and *somna* take a bit more thought, perhaps, but are related to English words such as 'somnambulist' (sleep walker), and so can be glossed initially as forms of the verb 'to sleep.' If we plug these in, the note begins to make more sense. The items that remain foreign at this stage are in italics.

> Hello Gunny! *Jeg* exit. Apology for absence. Too much temperature in *dies rummet* for sleep *als* eternal. *Jeg reviendra par middago.* Sleep *vohl!* Love, Flavia.

If even just a little Norwegian, German, Dutch and Italian (or Spanish) are known, these items are unproblematic. *Jeg* is 'I'; *dies* 'this'; *rummet* 'room'; *als* 'as'; *reviendra* 'return'; *par* 'for' or 'by'; *middago* 'midday'; and *vohl* 'well'.[11] Even if these languages are not known, the context of the note (something dashed off quickly to someone we live with), in combination with some of the phonetic similarities to existing English words (*dies*/this; *rummet*/room) allow for some intelligent guesses to be made. The note now looks like this:

> Hello Gunny! I exit. Apology for absence. Too much temperature in this room for sleep as eternal. I return for midday. Sleep well! Love, Flavia.

Fully translated, the note might read something like this:

> Hello Gunny! I've gone out. Sorry I'm not here. It is too hot in this room to sleep, as always. I'll be back by midday. Sleep well! Love, Flavia.

Flavia's note introduces some key grammatical morphemes (the personal pronoun *jeg*, the demonstrative *dies*, the prepositions *fur* and *par*) and a strategy for dealing with lexical morphemes, the semantic content words such as *eterno* (compare them with the existing English terms that they resemble). Additional uses of spEEC not only advance the story, but also provide further decoding opportunities. In a number of cases, for example, co-textual translations that reinforce the terms and strategies introduced in Flavia's note are supplied, such as 'If I'm lucky, Rosie. Ven jeg fortunato' (81). The translation in this piece of dialogue demonstrates a consistent use of *jeg* for *I*, and provides a way to work out the meaning of *fortunato*. The form of this spEEC term suggests *fortune* or *fortunate*, and the translation supports this gloss by pairing it with the English term *lucky*. With *jeg* and *fortunato* accounted for, *ven*, close to *when*, can then be equated with *if*. The spEEC words for 'nice' (*prettig*), 'see' (*videora*), and 'you' (*vous*) are similarly introduced when Gunpat greets Abe, a fellow smuggler, in both English and spEEC: 'Hello Abe, nice to see you again so soon. Prettig to videora vous. Nix somna?' (87). Gunpat's tendency to translate in this way also helps to convey his attitude about spEEC. While he will use it when he has to, he prefers English.

Repeated uses of spEEC also support comprehension. An initially confusing term, *wir* is gradually disambiguated in a series of clauses distributed over several pages, such as:

> Wir nix kaput yet, Schimt! (90)
> Wir transportera unser kommodities nach ein neu hide-out; (90)
> Feleich wir donatera Cancer Thouars die cut-out dopple-cross! (92)

As these examples make clear, *wir*, in at least one of its senses,[12] is the equivalent of *we're*. When taken together, such repeated uses can be compared with the illustrative examples often found in foreign language learning textbooks. Other pronouns are also presented this way:

> elle restera hier in Papeete? (81) / She will stay here in Papeete?
> Jeg restera hier unt dekoyera die Politzei (90) / I will stay here and decoy the Police.

Woven into and distributed throughout the dialogue, these paradigms are instructive without becoming intrusive.[13]

As this chapter has clearly shown, *Firefly*, *Otherland*, and 'Konfrontation' are stylistically innovative. All three texts eschew straightforwardness of delivery in favour of stylistic experimentation by directly representing contact phenomena in their dialogue. This is not done frivolously; rather, these experiments in style are offered to challenge what Clute (2003: 66) has called sf's 'old story', the largely 'First World vision . . . about the future written by inhabitants of, and for the benefit of readers who were inhabitants of, the industrialized Western World' (66). *Firefly*, *Otherland* and 'Konfrontation' use language contact phenomena to make English itself strange, demonstrating appropriation of the language at the character-character level of discourse, and abrogation of the English-only or English-dominant assumption at the text-audience/reader level.

What these texts forecast through style turns out to be a reasonable extrapolation. All three texts address questions that linguist themselves are asking about future English, questions succinctly summarized by David Crystal:

> What will be the balance of power among the major nations of the world a century from now? Will American supremacy continue to underwrite the role of English? Or will some momentous political or economic event motivate people to look elsewhere for their world language? (Crystal 1990: 274)

All three texts suggest shifts in the global balance of power; all three texts propose 'momentous political or economic event[s]', to echo Crystal (1990), that result in the birth of new lingua francas that de-status English; and *Otherland* and *Firefly* confront the issue of continued American supremacy in linguistic as well as other matters. 'Konfrontation', *Firefly* and *Otherland* offer visions of future Englishes that forecast language contact as a more salient reality than is currently the case for many speakers in the mother-tongue English nations. The end of the English-dominated era that so many of us now enjoy is, according to all of these texts, nearer than we may think. As Graddol (interviewed in Erard 2008: 31) has noted, non-native speakers of English, estimated to reach two billion world-wide by 2010, vastly outnumber native speakers, whose numbers are expected to fall from 350 million to 300 million by 2020. And while Crystal

(1990: 275) suggests that a de-regionalized international English may well emerge as a global lingua franca, he also notes that this is likely to sit alongside a proliferation of local Englishes (Indian, Caribbean, etc.) that are contact-influenced and mutually unintelligible.

Political and economic developments also favour the outcomes proposed in the three texts analysed here. As Csicsery-Ronay (2002: 220) notes, the power of nation-states and their national languages appears to be on the wane, 'undermined to an unprecedented degree by the driving institutions of the postmodern world.' As Csicsery-Ronay goes on to explain,

> the Internet, global capital markets, multinational corporations, the commodification of all cultural practices in global market terms, and social movements sophisticated in communications technologies have vitiated most of the attractive most of the attractive energies of national identification. (2002: 220)

Like Hinnenkamp (2003: 13), Csicsery-Ronay (2002) also notes that significant populations increasingly live cross-border lives, a circumstance that further weakens the notion 'of a nation as a homogenous population residing in a defined territory administered by the national state' (Csicsery-Ronay 2002: 220). 'Konfrontation', *Firefly* and *Otherland* participate in what Hinnenkamp (2003: 13) calls a 'hybridity discourse' by proposing just these kinds of worlds in their narratives, and extending their representation straight through to the kinds of contact-induced language change that can be expected to occur in such circumstances. In doing so, all three stand as a challenge to the still widely held view that alternative world texts either avoid or misuse experiments in form.

The question that remains, of course, is whether or not the texts studied here are exceptional in their representation of contact phenomena, or indicative of a more general trend in alternative world texts. The prevailing view of style in alternative world fiction would classify them as exceptional. Meyers (1980: 19), for instance, claimed that representations of contact phenomena were rare. Citing assertions made by Friend (1973: 998–9), he complained about textual short cuts, such as using contemporary English as though it were a future English with a nod and a wink to the reader, or stating that characters were speaking an altered English, but keeping the dialogue the isomorphic with the reader's English (e.g. *'Go away!' she said in High Englic*) (Meyers 1980: 20, 34). Meyers' (1980) take on the subject seems to have set the tone for future discussions. Stockwell (2000) and Hardy (2003) agree with him, and Crystal (2004/2005: 510) trots out what is essentially the same position.

In many science fiction works, for example, we would get the impression that time, linguistically, stands still. A spaceship leaves Earth for some distant star, and the author takes pains to deal with the problems of life maintenance and transmission as time passes between the generations; yet the language of the emigrants somehow remains exactly the same when they reach the star as when they left. (Crystal 2004/2005: 510)

While I have not, of course, demonstrated that representations of language contact are frequent in alternative world fiction with my analysis of the three texts studied here, neither have commentators such as Meyers (1980), Stockwell (2000) and Crystal (2004/2005) definitively demonstrated paucity. More often, the rarity of contact phenomena is asserted and then texts chosen for study are positioned as exceptions (e.g. see Hardy 2003; Meyers 1980: 18; Stockwell 2000). Whether the representation of contact phenomena in alternative world fiction is rare or reasonably frequent thus remains an open question. What is clear is that it is time to rethink the *assumption* that it is rare. As more and more studies on alternative world fiction are done, the 'exceptions' seem to be mounting up. Consider also that the recently published *Encyclopedia of Fictional and Fantastic Languages* (Conley and Cain 2006) devotes a category, 'Syncretic/polylingual languages', to contact phenomena and covers about a dozen works (including *Blade Runner*, the 2004 film *Code 46*, and Lovecraft's 'The Rats in the Walls'). Typically considered exceptions, representations of contact phenomena in alternative world texts may instead by the tip of the iceberg.

Chapter 3

Evoking the Past

The previous chapter looked at textually represented future Englishes and demonstrated that style played an essential role in not only
disrupting the language of the text for thematically relevant purposes, but in ensuring that these disruptions were still understandable. Here is in this chapter, we consider another kind of thematically
relevant linguistic distortion, the use of archaic forms. Five texts are
studied, Stephen Baxter's *Conqueror* (*Time's Tapestry Book Two*, 2007);
Cecilia Dart-Thornton's *The Lady of the Sorrows* (*The Bitterbynde Trilogy
Book Two*, 2002, hereafter *Lady*); Michael Moorcock's *Elric* (Gollancz's
Fantasy Masterworks edition[1]; Robert E. Howard's *Conan the
Adventurer*[2] (hereafter *Conan*); and Dunsany's *The King of Elfland's
Daughter* (1924/1969, hereafter *Elfland*). These texts span some
80 years, from 1924 to the present, and represent important mile-
stones in the development of alternative world texts. Dunsany's work
is an early and influential exponent of modern fantasy as we have
come to know it today (Carter 1973: viii; Schweitzer 1997: 121), the
Conan stories are representative of the pulp era, Moorcock's *Elric*
is widely acknowledged as a signature 'new wave' creation, and *Conqueror* and *Lady* represent current trends in alternative world fiction.

Archaic forms, generally called archaisms, are words or constructions retained from an earlier period of the language but no longer
in general use (definition after Baldick 1990: 16; Traugott and Pratt
1980: 114; Leech 1969: 13; Crystal 1964). Examples typically cited
include the second person singular pronouns (*thou, thee*), the – *(e)st*
and *-eth* verb inflections (*Hearest thou? / He heareth*); and irregular
forms such as *spake* (Leech 1969: 13; Crystal 1964). Mostly associated
with poetry 'from Spenser to Hardy' (Baldick 1990: 16, see also Leech
1969: 14; Richardson 1994; Elfenbein 2008: 84), their popularity has,

since the early years of the twentieth century, 'petered out' (Leech 1969: 14) and they are these days often considered something of a 'superficial pretence' (Sonmez 2002).

Guides to literary study, interesting in this regard for how they package and promote widely accepted views, assert that archaisms are 'rare in prose' (quote from Cuddon 1998: 53, see also Baldick 1990: 16). But as even a quick glance through the pages of many alternative world texts will reveal, archaic forms occur in abundance in this type of prose. Alternative world texts are, in fact, one of the few places where archaic forms survive. They occurred in all but one of the texts studied in this chapter, and manifested at multiple levels of analysis.[3] At the lexical level, for example, swords were *girt* (*Conan* 54), enemies were *slain* (*Conan* 56), and sometimes lovers (*Elric* 26) and brothers (*Conan* 60); adversaries would *smite* one another (*Elric* 13; *Elfland* 226; *Conan* 57, 76), runes were *besought* (*Elfland* 220). Characters were *bade* to do things (*Elfland* 4) in some places, and *wont* to do things of their own accord in others (*Elfland* 215) and, either way, might do things *anon* (*Lady* 165). They would *hearken* to one another (*Lady* 101, 112, 265) and what they were desirous of they would *fain* do (*Lady* 165, 300). Fields were *wolds* (*Elfland* 150) and full of *beeves* (*Elfland* 198), the moon was 'at the *neap*' (the phase during which the tides are least extreme) (*Elfland* 222), twilight was *the gloaming* (*Elfland* 14), and the nights were *fell* (terrible, cruel, deadly) (*Lady* 375). Archaic meanings were also revived in these texts, such as the sense of 'appropriate or fitting for *meet*, as in 'meet for derision' (*Elfland* 196), and 'meet to bear oneself like a Queen' (*Lady* 264–5). *Must* in the earlier sense of *may* or *might* also occurred: 'were that a more prevalent condition, mortalkind must find itself in better state' (*Lady* 380), as did 'fate or ultimate judgement' for *doom*: 'they must have thought my doom sealed' (*Conan* 117); 'my role, my destiny, my doom'; 'I know your doom'; 'my doom is near me, I think' (*Elric* 317, 217, 103). *Without* was used as the opposite of *within*: 'within your house or without it' (*Lady* 88); 'those wolves howling without' (*Conan* 41); and *seethe* was used in its original sense of 'boil': 'the oceans seethe', 'the ground began to *seethe*' (*Elric* 57, 245, italics in the original).

Archaic grammatical forms find ready expression in many works of alternative world fiction, as well. In the texts studied here, the

second person singular pronouns were represented in their subjec-
tive (*thou art a legend* [*Elric* 205]; *thou has won this game* [*Lady* 501];
thou speakest [*Lady* 501]) and objective forms (*I command thee – open*
[*Elric* 24]; *if pity moves thee* [*Lady* 310]; *we will go with thee* [*Conan* 58]).
Archaic possessive forms occurred as determiners, (*thy strength*
[*Elric* 182]; *thy little maid* [*Lady* 413]; *thine aid* [*Elric* 224, 328], *thine eyes*
[*Lady* 268]), and archaic reflexives were also evident ('[he] slung
over *him* by a strap a bottle of good new leather' [*Elfland* 9]).

Also evident were the *–(e)st* and *–eth* inflections (*your parliament saith*
[*Elfland* 1]; *anything song hath said* [*Elfland* 144]; *unholy horn doth sound*
[*Elric* 187]; *didst thou* [*Lady* 268]; *so thou sayest* [*Lady* 269]), imperatives with stated subjects (*know you this*; *go you then*; *begone you creatures*
[*Elric* 377, 389, 196]; *stay you Roxborough* [*Lady* 298]), and impersonal
expressions, such as *methought* (*Elric* 384; *Lady* 50, 54), *methinks* (*Lady*
57, 178), and various forms of *it pleases* (*Lady* 126, 149, 355). The verb
let also occurred archaically with *one* instead of the more modern *us*
or *me* (*Let one of you speak* [*Conan* 53] (see Greenbaum and Quirk
1990: 243). In addition, archaic prepositions were found (*unto this*
day [*Elfland* 3]; *wounded unto death* [*Conan* 117]; *did they teach you of it*
[*Elric* 41]), as well as a cluster of older adverbials and demonstratives
(*which he had hunted hither* [*Elfland* 135]; *who sent you hither* [*Elric* 200];
wither he had been dashed [*Conan* 76]; *and thence, hideously to the earth*
[*Conan* 188]; *news to take you hence* [*Elric* 59]; *go hence* [*Elfland* 213];
whence it came [*Elric* 387]; *whence so few ever returned* [*Elfland* 15]; *whence*
the sounds came [*Conan* 99]; *the grave mound you see yonder* [*Elric* 384];
yonder steps [*Elric* 67]; *yonder mansion* [*Elric* 398]; *yon child* [*Lady* 355]).

Archaic forms can also be considered deviant forms. While they
occur from time to time in educated native speaker usage it is difficult, as Minugh (1999) has argued, to consider them a productive
feature of modern standard English (see also Davidson 1997 and
Crystal 1964). Their use frequently entails obsolete syntax at odds
with what present day standard English requires or allows. This can
also be amply demonstrated with examples from the alternative world
texts explored here. Verbs and subjects can occur in clause final
positions (*unsavoury louts they were* [*Elric* 234]; *a name you will need*
[*Lady* 15]; *terrible was the revenge* [*Lady* 135]), and verbs can precede
subjects (*alone would roam this witch* [*Elfland* 3]; *high soared the dragon*

[*Elric* 188]). Single modifiers can follow rather than precede the nouns they modify, as in *all things true* (*Elfland* 4); *a field untended* (*Elfland* 13); *Champion Eternal* (*Elric* 244, 384), *accents unfamiliar* (*Lady* 477), and co-ordinated adjectives can be postposed (Crystal 1964: 152) to yield examples such as *clever fighters, and well-disciplined* (*Elric* 214). Questions can occur without auxiliary *do* where present-day English would require it (*Speak you so to the conquerors of the world?* [*Elric* 179]; *Fear'st thou that?* [*Lady* 277]; *How fares our master?* [*Elfland* 107], as can negatives (*look not askance* [*Lady* 111]; *speak not too hastily* [*Elric* 108]; *let not the two touch* [*Elfland* 184]; *I know not* [*Conan* 117].

The simple present (e.g. *a storm comes*) can be used to express progressive meanings (e.g. *a storm is coming*), for example, *the Chaos fleet comes* (*Elric* 335), *I bleed* (*Lady* 244), and *why do you follow me?* (*Conan* 174). In addition, the perfective aspect, which is formed with the auxiliary verb *to have* in present day English, can occur with *to be* instead, as in *the time was come* (*Elfland* 91); *the parliament of Erl was met* (*Elfland* 123), *I am come* (*Lady* 459), *the herald was gone southwards* (*Elric* 222). Modal auxiliaries can occur as full verbs (*I must away and instruct my men* [*Elric* 290]; *you must out with it* [*Lady* 74]; *I'll to bed now* [*Elric* 320], a straightforward violation of modern English which classifies modals only as auxiliaries (constructions such as *she must the house* are impossible). Similarly, passive voice constructions which in today's English would require a form of the verb *to have*, such as *They have been killed*, can occur as they once did with a form of *to be* instead (*Huon is driven forth!* [*Lady* 244]; *you are discovered* [*Lady* 195]; *is the prophecy explained?* [*Elric* 232]. Expressions in the subjunctive mood that are deviant in today's English also occurred in the texts investigated here. The subjunctive in present-day English is mostly limited to dependent *that*-clauses (*She insists that he walk to work; he prefers that she be on time*); a few fixed phrases (*Heaven forbid, suffice it to say, God Bless*, etc.); and, in the past, to 'were' in conveying hypotheticals, conditionals, and wishes (*Suppose everyone were rich; If I were you, I would start now; I wish I were younger*) (Burrow and Turville-Petre 2005: 48–9; Greenbaum and Quirk 1990: 44). The alternative world texts studied here, however, re-expanded the subjunctive in keeping with some of its earlier uses. The present tense *be*-subjunctive, for example, was used in a range of conditional contexts that would be more comfortably expressed with *is, are* or *am* today:

if we be but a day away from our kind we are lonely; (*Elfland* 15)

however it be, all those that have come by a magical sword, have always felt that joy; (*Elfland* 9)

though you *be* of Chaos; (*Elric* 378)

whether you be within your house or without it. (*Lady* 88)

Examples of the past subjunctive, mostly overtaken in modern English by the use of modal verbs (Burrow and Turville-Petre 1992/2005: 49–50), were also found. *Elfland* provides several such instances, where *were* is used in place of present-day English *would be*, such as *darkness were better now that Elfland was gone* (84); *if darkness had lain forever upon those angular rocks it were better* (84), and *had he let them have their way there were no trolls left in Elfland* (167). Such constructions are closer to various Middle English uses of *were* that Burrow and Turville-Petre (1992/2005: 49) cite than to present-day English (e.g. '[*to have*] *alle were þe better*', meaning *to have all would be better*).

Finally, consider various hypotheticals and conditionals that were expressed with *had* where present-day English would use a construction with *would have* (Greenbaum and Quirk 1990: 66; Burrow and Turville-Petre 1992/2005: 49):

And now a watcher in the marshes, if such there had been, *had seen* something more than a traveller; (*Elfland* 205)

A watcher, if there had been one . . . *had noticed* after a while; (*Elfland* 204)

. . . no eye *had seen* him unless it were gazing already at the spot at which he appeared; (*Elfland* 43)

Had it not been for that chance jam roll she *had gone* to Elfland; (*Elfland* 49)

And were he not the King . . . he *had wept*. (*Elfland* 39)

While these were especially prevalent in *Elfland*, they also occurred in *Lady* (*had not the King-Emperor come to succor us we* had *all perished*,

259; *had you but confided to me this tale of treasure troves, thou* hadst *saved thyself a deal of toil,* 268–9).

In their deviance, archaic forms are a departure from the plain, ordinary language that is, as noted in Chapter 1, repeatedly said to characterize alternative world texts. Irwin's (1976) articulation of this view is perhaps the most extreme. Since, he says, fantasy's primary goal is to persuade, it must convey its fantastic content in straightforward, ordinary, easy-to-accept language. According to Irwin (1976), 'purposeful distortions are noticeably absent' (79) from fantasy, and fantasy authors 'ordinarily stay within Standard English' (Irwin 1976: 194). Clearly, given the examples above, such a view of style in alternative world texts is too narrow. Deviant archaisms not only occur in alternative world fiction, but play a significant role. They can be an effective means of distancing the alternative world of the text from the reader's own (Le Guin 1973/1993: 85, see also Richardson 1994, who makes a similar point about archaic forms in romantic poetry), and can be instrumental in bringing a coherent past world to life in the narrative.

Such textual animations of the past are an acknowledged feature of many alternative world texts, particularly secondary world fantasies, which are often set in a 'pseudo' – (Hunt, in Hunt and Lenz 2001/2004: 4), 'quasi' – (Thompson 1982: 215), or 'vaguely medieval' time period (Zanger 1982: 230, see also Attebery 1992: 109; Carter 1973: 8; Manlove 1975: 8; and Sullivan 1996: 312). The role of archaic forms in this project, however, is seldom appreciated. Instead, as Sullivan (1996: 304) has noted, critical energies have largely been spent on 'enumerating the traditional sources on which high fantasy has drawn for its reality' (see, for example, Cantrell 1981; Reynolds 1987; Swinfen 1984: 82–3; Thompson 1982; Zanger 1982). The effective use of accurate historical and archaeological data has also been of interest (e.g. see Reynolds 1987), although such accounts sometimes include deprecatory comments about the supposedly many (but unnamed) authors who 'lack the depth of antiquarian knowledge that allowed Tolkien or Morris to roam freely in a reconstructed medieval world' (Attebery 1992: 132–3), or who depend on second-hand borrowing of historical detail (Reynolds 1987: 10).

When archaic forms are given explicit attention, the focus tends to be on tracing their derivations (e.g. Parker 1956; Shippey 1982; Tinkler 1968) or historical literary precedents (Anderson 1988; Pfeiffer 1979; Swinfen 1984: 86; Ugolnik 1977). Connors (2001) offers some potentially interesting work on the archaic dialect used in Lovecraft's 'The Picture in the House' (1920), noting that it serves to establish character, and expresses one of Lovecraft's enduring themes, humanity's complex interaction with time. However, Connors' (2001) observations on archaic dialect features are not supported by any linguistic analysis. Not one example of the archaic dialect represented in the story is given. Instead, Connors (2001) relies on previous work, Eckhardt (1991), similarly non-linguistic in focus, and Lovecrafts's own views as expressed in interviews and letters. Other accounts have been subjective. Wilson (1984) was impressed by E. R. Eddison's use of archaic language, but did not say much about why. Delany (1976/1977) was unimpressed with archaic forms, but his comments amount to brief remarks: '[t]raditionally, sword and sorcery is written with a sort of verbal palette knife – an adjective-heavy exclamatory diction that mingles myriad archaisms with other syntactical distortions meant to signal the antique: the essence of the pulps' (214).

While archaic forms in alternative world texts are appreciated and valued by some commentators, views like Delany's are more common. Archaic forms are by wider reputation considered 'clumsy and affected' as Anderson (1988: 11) points out, and 'less palatable to modern tastes' (Wilson 1984: 13). They can be, it is sometimes thought, 'difficult to read' (Irwin 1987: 46), 'a tough sell for the modern reader' (Chadbourne 2008: 10), 'elaborate' and not always 'worth the effort' (Hume 1984: 166). In part, this may be due to their more general depreciation. As noted earlier, their popularity, among both writers and critics, has tailed off considerably since the end of the nineteenth century (Leech 1969: 14). It might also be due to their frequent use in, and association with, sword and sorcery. As Hunt and Lenz (2004: 2), de Camp (1976), and Carter (1973: 147, 157–8) have all noted, this sub-genre has come in for severe criticism (not all of it fair), and even critics otherwise well-disposed towards alternative world fiction have sought to distance themselves from it (e.g. see Attebery 1992: 2, 9; Le Guin 1973/1993: 81; Mobley 1973).

Whatever the reason, it is time to re-assess the literary use of archaic language, a point that Sonmez (2002) has made in relation to the use of archaic forms in Coleridge's 'The Rime of the Ancient Mariner'. 'When a writer distributes archaic material throughout his work,' suggests Somnez (2002), 'the reader understands that the whole of that work is meant seemingly to belong to the time when such material was normally found.' That archaic forms are not, strictly speaking, authentic, does not negate their effectiveness. As Sonmez (2002) explains, archaisms used atavistically tend to be far more regular in form than they were in original use, and they also tend to be 'chronologically contradictory', with forms appearing together that were in actual fact separated by centuries. The point, however, as Thompson (1982) notes, is not to document the past but to suggest it, and in this archaic forms can be effective. As Sonmez (2002) has suggested, archaic forms work metonymically: small traces of the past, such as old words or grammatical forms evoke 'the invisible presence or influence of the whole'. They are, in essence, textual '"wormholes"' (Sonmez 2002) that pull readers from their present into the past world of the narrative.

An investigation of these textual 'wormholes' along pragmatic lines provides further insight into how alternative world texts can establish a persuasive textual past in the reader's present. A pragmatic analysis, in the main, is interested not in how a language is structured, but in how actual speakers use a given language. Studies in pragmatics, for example, look at how people have conversations, how they design their utterances for their interlocutors, how they know when and when not to speak, about what, and to whom, in any given situation. The field of historical pragmatics, a relatively young discipline that only began to take shape in the mid-1990s (Mazzon 2009: 1), is interested in how a particular language has been used by its speakers in different stages of its historical development. Developing out of contrastive pragmatics (Jacobs and Jucker 1995; Mazzon 2009: 1), historical pragmatics compares pragmatic features as realized in different time periods of the same language (e.g. apologies in Old

English and Early Modern English) rather than in different languages or varieties of the same period (e.g. complaints in present-day German and English). It conducts its investigations largely by looking for pragmatic phenomena classified in studies of contemporary talk in texts from earlier periods (Jacobs and Jucker 1995: 5). Typically, the texts of central interest are written accounts of spoken events, such as courtroom proceedings; texts written to be spoken, such as sermons and speeches; and texts meant to imitate speech, such as literary works and language teaching dialogues (see Jacobs and Jucker 1995; Mazzon 2009).

The analyses undertaken in this chapter might be considered to fall within the field of applied historical pragmatics in that I have used findings from historical pragmatics to further the interpretation of present day literary texts set in the past. For example, I compared Middle and Early Modern English realizations of speech acts identified by studies in historical pragmatics (e.g. Mazzon 2009; Palander-Collin 2009) with their representations in the alternative world texts studied here and found a reasonable degree of correspondence. This was especially evident with greetings, leave-takings, expressions of gratitude and exclamations. In keeping with older English usage (e.g. see Mazzon 2000, 2009), characters said, for example, 'Hail to thee, Lord' (*Lady* 49); 'Greetings, Lord Elric' (*Elric* 7); and 'Greetings, King Guthran' (*Elric* 135) when they met. When taking their leave of each other, they said 'Farewell my lord, and be lucky' (*Elric* 163); 'Fare you well, then, my friend' (*Elric* 380); and 'Fare *you* well, good cousin' (*Elric* 380). In gratitude, they said 'Gramercie. I am weary' (*Lady* 47) and 'Gramericie m'lady' (*Lady* 206). In frustration, they exclaimed 'Fie!'; 'Zounds!', and 'Pon my troth!' (*Lady* 119, 91, 374, 112). The strength, or force, or a speech act can be modified, as Brown and Levinson (1978/1987) have noted, either softened with a hedging device or aggravated with an intensifier. Early English realizations of these devices, such as *pray* to mitigate imperatives (Mazzon 2009: 133) and forms of *sooth* or *verily* to intensify (Lenker 2007: 82), were also evident (*pray conduct her Ladyship to them with due consideration* [*Lady* 48]; *Pray, do not think me unkind* [*Lady* 47]; *In sooth, she will have* [*Lady* 12]; *Yeah, verily m'lady* [*Lady* 55].

When studied in relation to findings from historical pragmatics, lines of dialogue such as 'pon my troth' are not gratuitous affectations but genuine archaisms. Like their lexical and grammatical counterparts, they establish through-ways to the past for the imagination. They are, however, also important for another reason. Archaic speech act formulae not only open a door to the past, but suggest a community of speakers who naturally inhabit that past world. As Taavitsainen and Jucker (2007) have noted, speech acts 'are culture-specific and time-specific', and every community has its own distinct 'inventory of speech acts' (108). Acts such as greetings or leave-takings, inter-personal rituals as Goffman (1967) called them, can be especially telling. They are often formulaic, and these formulae are explicitly recognized as characteristic of particular communities. Familiar to many speakers of present-day English, for example, will be expressions such as *Hi there; Hey; What's up* and *See ya; Take care; Bye now*. Exclamations, expressions of gratitude, and forms of address are similarly emblematic (e.g. *Oh, shit!, You're a star!, Excuse me*, etc.). These are specific to our time and our culture(s) and sub-cultures. It is probably for this very reason that alternative world texts seeking to establish a coherent past world in their narratives avoid them. As just shown, it was the ritual and highly formulaic speech acts – the emblematic greetings, leave-takings, exclamations, and expressions of gratitude – that were most often expressed archaically in the texts studied here. As Dawson (2005: 108), through Tolkien (Carpenter, ed. 1981: 225–6) notes, characters wearing hauberks and helms and carrying shields need to speak accordingly. Archaic formulae, a feature of style, can help to create the illusion of a living past by presenting characters as active and participating members of an earlier speech community.

Archaic terms of address play a particularly important part in maintaining this illusion of a past speech community. Terms of address, as Levinson (1983: 89) has observed, encode speaker judgements about the social parameters of a speech situation (see also Stockwell 2000: 39). To address someone as Sir, for example, is not simply to identify, but to express attitudes of distance and/or respect, as well. Historically, terms of address were also socially indicative in this way, and investigating their use in a community can tell us something about the social structure of that community (Mazzon 2009: 19). As Nevalainen and Raumolin-Bronberg (1995) point out, studies of address terms in Middle and Early Modern English 'reveal a carefully graduated scale of social hierarchy' (547). A corresponding, and correspondingly revealing scale (as judged by the historical forms recorded in Mazzon 2009; Nevalainen and Raumolin-Bronberg 1995; and Palander-Collin 2009) was evident in the texts studied here. Noble and aristocratic characters were deferentially addressed according to rank (*Lord Elric* [*Elric* 7]; *the Lady Shaarilla* [*Elric* 52]; *Lord Donblas* [*Elric* 407]; *Lord Pyaray* [*Elric* 360]), and possessive determiners were frequently included in the addressing noun phrase (*my liege* [*Elric* 87]; *My Lord Ash* [*Lady* 96]; *Your Grace* [*Lady* 83]; *My lady* [*Lady* 53; *Elfland* 51]). Severe submission and extreme distance was shown by direct address in the third person (e.g. *Does my lady wish that I should soap her back* [*Lady* 52]). As it was in earlier Englishes (see Mazzon 2000: 149–50; Palander-Collin 2009: 57), polite address among strangers was indicated with *master, sir, friend,* or the use of one's occupation as a title, often accompanied by *good* or *dear* (*good sir* [*Elric* 52]; *good master* [*Elric* 51]; *good Freer* [*Elfland* 29]; *Master* [*Elfland* 179]). Kinship terms (*father, brother, sister,* etc.) were often used as terms of intimate address in earlier Englishes (Mazzon 2009), and this pattern also found expression in the alternative world texts investigated here. The king's sister Yasmina in 'The People of the Black Circle' is known by her title to just about everyone, but *sister* to the king (*Aie, save me, my sister!* [*Conan* 14]), and the king in turn to her is *brother* (*Brother! . . . I am here!* [*Conan* 12]). Similarly, Elric addresses one of his royal relatives as *good cousin* (380). In *Conan, Elric, Lady* and *Elfland,* terms of address are realized archaically not simply as individual tokens. They take part in a pattern of address that is also archaic. Terms such as *Lord, good sir,* and *my lady* are not just quaint words, but active distinctions in a textually re-animated feudalism.[4]

Terms of address are also interesting here for their role in signalling intimacy and distance between interlocutors. As Brown and Levinson (1978/1987) have shown, terms of address in present-day English can be used to reflect existing states of intimacy or distance between speakers, or to indicate movement along this continuum (see also Chapter 2, page 44). They can also be used strategically. For example, an address term can invoke a relationship of intimacy to soften a command, or confer status to show deference (Brown and Levinson 1978/1987). Work in historical pragmatics has shown that address terms in earlier Englishes were similarly involved in signalling intimacy or distance (e.g. see Mazzon 2000, 2009; Nevalainen and Raumolin-Bronberg 1995; Palander-Collin 2009). In a number of the texts studied in this chapter, archaic forms of address signalled shifts in character relations that were not only essential to the story but also consistent with the social hierarchy established in the narratives. This again serves to present characters as active participants in a coherent speech community come to life from the past. An interesting example of this occurs in the first meeting between Elric and Moonglum, the man who is to become his co-adventurer and only true friend. They meet when Elric decides to aid Moonglum in a fight against a pack of vicious half-dog, half-bird creatures (50–1). At first, their speech is asymmetric. Elric greets Moonglum with *friend*, and Moonglum replies with *master* and *sir*.

Elric: 'Turn and stand, my friend – I'm here to aid you'; (50)
Moonglum: 'A lucky chance, this meeting, good master'; (51)
Moonglum: 'Thanks, good sir'. (52)

As their interaction continues, they move towards a more equal footing, speaking as respectful acquaintances:

'So you are from Elwher, Master Moonglum . . . You have ridden far.'
'Indeed I have, sir.' (53)

Moonglum, ignorant of Elric's reputation as treacherous kinslayer, is something of fresh start for Elric (52), who finds himself 'liking the man more and more' (53). When Moonglum suggests travelling together, Elric agrees: 'Very well then, friend Moonglum' (53). *Friend* in this instance, in combination with the first name, marks the start of the new friendship between Elric and 'his new-found companion' (53) (see Mazzon 2000: 150 and Palander-Collin 2009: 57 on the various historical uses of *friend*). In the meeting scene between Elric and Moonglum, the two characters move from the assumption of asymmetry, to respectful strangers, to friends, and this progression is indicated in the archaic address terms in a way that fits naturally with the stratified society represented in the narrative.

A similar progression is signalled in a rather more difficult meeting between Elric and his cousin, Dyvim Tvar, Lord of the Dragon Caves. The two become estranged after Elric's deadly treachery of his own family and people and when they meet again the conversation is somewhat awkward, to say the least. Their discomfort is marked in the language through the use of 'the age-old ritual greeting' (87), textually represented through the use of the archaic third person address, which stresses extreme distance:

Dyvim Tvar: 'Dyvim Tvar, Lord of the Dragon Caves, greets Elric, Master of Melniboné, Exponent of her Secret Arts.' (86)

Elric: 'Elric, Master of Melniboné, greets his loyal subject and demands that he give audience to Dyvim Tvar.' (87)

The third person address continues, marking the stiffness in the communication, and the characters' mutual distrust:

Dyvim Tvar: 'I would be honoured if my liege would allow me to accompany him to my pavilion.' (*Elric* 87)

The two proceed to Dyvim Tvar's tent, and Elric breaks a long silence, offering an acknowledgement of guilt, and a step towards intimacy by dropping the third person address:

'You know me for a betrayer, a thief, a murderer of my own kin and a slayer of my countrymen, Dragon Master.' (*Elric* 87)

Dyvim Tvar, still unconvinced, maintains distance:

'With my liege's permission, I will agree with him.' (*Elric* 87)

Elric makes another move towards solidarity with his cousin, and this time it is accepted, although reluctantly, when Dyvim Tvar switches from third person to second person (*you*).

> 'We were never so formal in the old days, when alone,' Elric said. 'Let us forget ritual and tradition –Melniboné is broken and her sons are wanderers. We meet, as we used to, as equals – only now, this is wholly true. We *are* equals. The Ruby Throne crashed in the ashes of Imrryr and now no emperor may sit in state.'
>   Dyvim Tvar sighed. 'This is true Elric – but why have you come here? [. . .]. (87)

From this point on, the men get down to the real business of the talk and hammer out an alliance.

In *Lady*, the growing friendship between the protagonist Rohain and her maid is also choreographed in archaic terms of address. When the maid first enters Rohain's service, she addresses Rohain with maximum submission and distance in the third person:

> 'Then shall I lay Her Ladyship's raiment for the evening?'; (52)
> 'My Lady already has the look that others wish to achieve – she
>   needs no paint.' (58)

Rohain at first preserves the symmetry, addressing the maid simply by name, *Viviana*. As time goes on, however, the relationship changes. Rohain, once in service herself, is humble and generous rather than pretentious. While the maid maintains respectful address with *m'lady* and similar terms, it is not long before she drops the third person address. The relationship moves swiftly from master-servant to friendship, and a very clear indication of this is when Rohain spontaneously begins to address her maid with the affectionate nickname *Via* (180).

Strategic uses of address terms are similarly consistent with the stratified past worlds represented in the texts. Consider, for example, a strategic use of *sir* in *Elric*. When the Lady Zarozinia, a noble-born character who is to become Elric's wife, first meets Moonglum her generosity of spirit is displayed when she elevates his status with respect to herself by addressing him as *Sir Moonglum.* In *Elfland,* Prince Alveric employs the kinship term *mother* strategically. When his half-human, half-elf child is born, he experiences some trouble getting a nurse to look after him. He turns to the witch Ziroonderel and mitigates his request by conferring intimacy: ' "Mother Witch", said Alveric, "will you come to the Vale of Erl and care for him and be the nurse at the castle?".'

As demonstrated, archaic forms in alternative world texts are neither rare nor superficial. They are not spurious or randomly occurring, but integral elements of the vocabulary, grammar and discourse that serve to create the illusion of a living past. As also demonstrated, archaic forms are deviant forms. They are not, as Lynch (2005: 81) has noted, part of the present-day English that authors and readers share (see also Sonmez 2002; Traugott and Pratt 1980), and they can pose barriers to understanding. Alternative world texts that disrupt the language of their own telling to suggest a past world in their narratives, have, like the futuristic stories discussed in Chapter 2, a delicate textual balancing act to achieve. That is, suggesting a past English poses a similar challenge to suggesting a future one. The language must be different enough from the reader's own to convince, but not so distant that we lose touch with the narrative. This balancing act becomes even more significant when we consider that many modern readers are not simply unaccustomed to archaic forms but, as Frye (1957, in Shippey 1982: 160) notes, positively schooled in the realist tradition, where language often seeks to reflect contemporary usage rather than increase distance from it.

To demonstrate how the texts studied here created past worlds without exiling readers of present-day English, we can look again at deviant clause patterns. These tend to be carefully poised between the demands of the archaic style on one hand, and the structure of present-day English on the other. One of the primary issues is ensuring that subjects and objects are clearly differentiated so that readers know who or what acts, and who or what gets acted upon. In present-day English, this is largely achieved through the order of elements. In a sentence such as *The dog saw the cat,* we know that it was *the dog* who did the seeing and *the cat* that was seen because *the dog* occurs before the verb, and *the cat* after it. If we change that we get either a different meaning, *The cat saw the dog*, or confusion, *Saw the cat the dog* (explanation after Culpeper 2005: 60). One way of ensuring that subject and object are not confused when disrupting the order of elements in the archaic style is to limit the disruption to clauses that naturally take no object. A sentence such as *Jane is nice*, for example, does not have a subject and an object, but a subject (Jane) and an attribute of that subject (*nice*, technically a subject complement). Such sentences can also express some equivalent of the subject, such as *Jane is a doctor*. In cases like these, the order of elements can be changed so that either the verb or the subject may occur in final position without loss of meaning (*Nice Jane is; A doctor is she*) because there is no object to be confused with the subject. Many of the examples found follow this pattern:

> unsavoury louts they were; (*Elric* 9)
> not like the runes that enraged the flames was the song she sang to
>   the sword; (*Elfland* 6)
> shrewd was he; (*Lady* 350)
> terrible ravagers were they; (*Lady* 245)
> rugged and rocky was the coastline. (*Lady* 579)

Another way to avoid confusion between subject and object is to limit clause element manipulations to those clauses with intransitive verbs, as these require no object (e.g. *the sun shines; the moon rose; the package arrived*). In such cases, the subject can occur in final position and is often further delayed by adverbials and modifiers:

> back through the guarding wood went Alveric and Lirazel;
>   (*Elfland* 26)
> so went Orion and his pack of hounds; (*Elfland* 150)
> then up spake a grizzled troll; (*Elfland* 164)
> high soared the dragon; (*Elric* 188)
> hilt-deep the sabre sank; (*Conan* 115)
> past the tower on its northern headland sailed the boat with its
>   passengers. (*Lady* 382)

Alternative world texts can also suggest older clause patterns by using devices of postponement that present-day English still allows.

When it is desirable, for reasons of focus or emphasis, for example, to mention the subject last, *there* can be inserted at the front of the clause in the ordinary position as a 'dummy' subject (Greenbaum and Quirk 1990: 425). Contrast, for instance, *A man is standing up* with *There is a man standing up* (see Greenbaum and Quirk 1990: 425 for further discussion). Alternative world fiction can make similar use of *there* to front the verb and echo the verb-subject word order typically used in Old English after adverbs such as 'then' and 'there' (Mitchell and Robinson 1992: 65, 68–9):

> there slipped a great white unicorn over the border; (*Elfland* 125)
> there rose another sound above the clash of steel and yells of slaughter; (*Conan* 87)
> there came an evening when the moon was almost full. (*Lady* 588)

This effect can be heightened by including adverbials that further separate the verb from the subject:

> there came up to him from far below, shrill and clear in the early morning, the sound of his peacocks calling; (*Elfland* 147)
> and at this time there met one day in the forge of Narl, all unknown to Orion, the men of the Parliament of Erl. (*Elfland* 114)

Stripped bare and put in a more idiomatic order, these sentences are: *The sound of his peacocks calling came up to him* and *The men of the Parliament of Erl met in the forge of Narl.* Postponing the subjects by inserting *there* allows the verbs to be positioned prior to the subjects and near the front of the clauses. The intervening material (*from far below, shrill and clear in the early morning; one day, all unknown to Orion*) serves to delay the subjects even further, emphasizing their clause-final positions.

Stephen Baxter's *Conqueror* illustrates how deviant lexis can be integrated so that the language of the text differs from the reader's own, but can still be understood. Set largely in Anglo-Saxon England between 607 and 1066, *Conqueror* revives and integrates obsolete Old English vocabulary to actualize its setting. Perhaps paradoxically, it is not the most extensive use of Old English in *Conqueror*, the 'invented prophecy' (Aranga 2007) in 'The Menologium of the Blessed Isolde' at the opening of the novel, that is the most effective. Comprising some two pages of continuous verse, this presents a considerable obstacle to comprehension, as few readers would be able to cope with such a long an unbroken stretch of Old English. This is, presumably, why readers are not obliged to cope with it. The modern English version is provided in full, allowing readers to skip the Old English version entirely if they wish. When the prophecy is discussed by the characters in the narrative itself, it is the modern English version that is used:

> 'The comet,' Wuffa breathed.
> 'Yes! And it is the comet around whose visits the prophecy is
>   structured.' In a quavering voice Ambrosias began to read:
> These the Great Years / of the Comet of God
> Whose awe and beauty / in the roof of the world [. . .]. (Baxter 34)

More interesting, and more effective, is when the illusion of spoken Old English is evoked through the accumulated, and seemingly casual, uses of Old English vocabulary (e.g. *scop, witan, seax, atheling*). In many ways, Baxter's integration of obsolete Old English into a present-day English text is similar to the integration of non-English vocabulary in works of post-colonial fiction by authors such as Chinua Achebe. What is celebrated in post-colonial fiction (e.g. see Ashcroft et al. 1989), however, is dismissed or seldom noticed when it occurs in alternative world texts.

Old English words in *Conqueror* are often used to refer to Anglo-Saxon cultural practices, artefacts and beliefs that have no comfortable expression in our own English. Definitions of the terms are seamlessly integrated into the narrative without intrusive 'expository lumps':

> . . . a *scop*, a wandering poet, called at his home village; (16)
> He stood his ground, his hand hovering at the hilt of his *seax*, his
>   bone-handled knife; (8)
> But in this *burh*, this fortified place. (162)

In other cases, translations are briefly integrated:

> 'You refer to this island of yours, the part you own, as England.'
> *Engla-lond.* (136)
> 'And to yourselves as English.' *Englisc;* (136)
> 'Ut! Ut!' Out! Out!; (257)
> 'My father is on the *witan.* The King's Council'; (93)
> 'You are of the *wealisc.*' Welsh; (60)
> The ale, which the Germans call *beor,* was sweet and lumpy. (102)

Sometimes, meanings are clear from the context, as with *fyrd* in the example below:

> Cynewulf shook his head. 'How is it that we fall like straw men before mere hundreds?'
>
> 'Few of us are warriors,' Arngrim said. 'The thegns are raised to fight. But the fyrd are farmers. And when the harvest is due they melt away anyhow. These Danes are blooded warriors.' (143)

While fyrd may initially be confusing, neighbouring terms such as 'blooded', 'warriors', 'fight', and the wider context of talk about one of the Danish invasions, invite the (correct) meaning of some sort of conscripted army (Atherton 2006).

Another strategy used is to place characters in the position of explaining to each other something that readers also need to know. In the example below Macson, descended from the native Britons (in what is today Wales), explains an Anglo-Saxon belief to Belisarius, a book dealer from Constantinople. Along the way, readers discover the Old English term and concept of *wyrd.*

> Macson said, 'The Germans have a notion they call *wyrd.* Like fate – but vaguer, more entangling. They believe the Romans were brought low because they had desecrated the god-throttled landscape, because it was their time to go – because of *wyrd.* Now the Germans are building their own kingdoms. But they believe the must live well, or *wyrd* will do for them in their turn.' (74)

Macson also describes some Anglo-Saxon politics to Belisarius, and in so doing happens to explain *bretwalda* for the 'overhearing' readers:

> Macson shook his head. 'For decades much of the German country has been under the sway of Offa of Mercia. The other German kings recognise him as *bretwalda*, over-king.' (61)

Wergild, as both word and concept, is introduced the same way as Ammanius, a Romanized-Briton, asks Wuffa, a Saxon, about his people in a (mostly vain) attempt to understand them.

> Ammanius: 'You actually put a cost on a man's life, don't you? A penalty to be paid if one takes it?'
> Wuffa: 'We call it the *wergild*.' (22–3)

Anglo-Saxon naming practices are also indirectly revealed to the reader in this way. As Atherton (2006: 9) points out, Old English personal names are commonly 'dithematic', built from two independently meaningful elements. *Aelfflad*, for example, is *aelf* (elf or supernatural) + *flaed* (beauty). What is reference information about an old language to us is presented as living and consequential knowledge for the characters:

> 'Oh, I believe in Alfred. He may babble on about God, but he is the descendent of Woden after all, and he has a deeper wisdom than any priest. Think about his name.'
>   Alfred – *Aelf-red* – the wisdom of the elves. (163)

Names in *Conqueror* demonstrate another strategy for establishing a sense of Anglo-Saxon times within the confines of present-day English. Strictly speaking, many of the names used, both for people (e.g. *Cnyewulf, Aelfric, Aethelnoth; Elfgar, Leofgar, Aethelred, and Aelfflaed*) and places (*Eoforwic, Hamptonscir, Aescesdun, Brycgstow, Haestingaceaster, Sumorsaete*) are *Anglo-Saxonized*. That is, they are only as faithful to their Old English spellings as present-day English allows. Old English letters and digraphs no longer in use, such as thorn (þ), eth (ð) and ash (æ) are modernized to *th* and *ae* so that, for example,

`Æþelræd – unreadable in present-day English – becomes *Aethelred.* Where unfamiliar symbols are not at issue, however, original spellings are retained. For example, the sequence *sc* in Old English represented the first sound in *ship*, and this is retained in the spellings of place names such as Ae*sc*æsdun and Hampton*sc*ir. Similarly, *cg* represented the final sound in *bridge*, retained in Bry*cg*stow.[5] Retaining old spellings that can still be rendered in present-day English in small, manageable units such as single words allows for *Conqueror* to train its readers, who can use the provided key to place names, or their own familiarity with them, to work out, for example, that *Aescesdun* is Ashdown. Translations provided within the text, such as *English* and *Welsh* for *Englisc* and *Wealisc*, further strengthen the correspondence. In essence, the style of the texts turns the readers into linguists by asking them to piece together elements of an unknown language from the clues provided.

Another way to distance the language of the text without sacrificing meaning is to vary the archaic style with a style that is neither overtly archaized, nor obviously situated during the writer's own place or time. This is often done by employing present-day English, but in a formal style. Formal English, as Crystal (1964) notes, tends to exclude current slang expressions, expletives, interjections, and conversational idioms, all elements that would immediately place the discourse in our time and context. Other common features include a tendency towards syntactic complexity, use of 'elevated' lexis and an avoidance of contractions (Crystal 1964). Shippey (1982: 167) characterizes this style as 'intermediate', noting that while it contains few archaisms, neither does it contain any telling features familiar from ordinary present-day English. Tolkien himself addressed the avoidance of contemporary speech forms in one of his letters (Carpenter, ed. 1981: 225–6), where he invites comparison of what he actually wrote with a possible modernized version (also discussed in Shippey 1982: 167 and Dawson 2005: 108). The text Tolkien quotes from *The Lord of the Rings* is this:

'Nay Gandalf!' said the king. 'You do not know your own skill in healing. It shall not be so. I myself will go to war, to fall in the front of the battle, if it must be. Thus shall I sleep better.'

The modernized version he gives to demonstrate its unsuitability reads like this:

> 'Not at all, my dear G. You don't know your own skill as a doctor. Things aren't going to be like that.
>
> I shall go to the war in person, even if I have to be one of the first casualties . . . I should sleep sounder in my grave like that rather than if I stayed at home.' (Tolkien 1955 in Carter, ed. 1981: 225)

While neither version employs deviant forms, the modernized one, in closing the distance between reader and text, is less effective in evoking a sense of the distant past.

The texts studied here often displayed an adept use of the intermediate style, as the following passage from *Elric* demonstrates. Here, Elric and his cousin are discussing the nature of a recent omen.

> 'What did it tell you, cousin?' Elric asked eagerly.
>
> 'It gave a puzzling message. While we had barely gone from the marshes of the mist, it came and perched on my shoulder and spoke in human tongue. It told me to come to Sequaloris and there I would meet my King. From Sequaloris we were to journey together to join Yishana's army and the battle, whether won or lost, would resolve the direction of our linked destinies thereafter. Do you make sense of that, Cousin?'
>
> 'Some,' Elric frowned. 'But come – I have a place reserved for you at the inn. I will tell you all I know over wine – if we can find a decent wine in this forsaken hamlet. I need help, Cousin, as much help as I can obtain, for Zarozinia has been abducted by supernatural agents and I have a feeling that this and the wars are but two elements in a greater play.' (*Elric* 208)

With the exception of 'Cousin' as an address form, archaic forms are not a feature in this passage. Distance from the reader's own temporal context is achieved by avoiding features that would be familiar from ordinary, present-day English. For example, contractions, even where expected, are not used (*I will tell you* occurs instead of *I'll tell you*) and elevated lexis replaces more ordinary terms (*puzzling* instead of *strange, perched* instead of *sat, journey* instead of *go, obtain* instead of *get*). The cumulative result of the intermediate style, as Shippey (1982: 67) notes, is an effective evocation of a past world. The modern world is kept at bay without stressing the reader with constant archaizing.

Speech acts concerning the time, seemingly hum-drum when first considered, also turn out to be an interesting demonstration of the intermediate style in alternative world fiction.[6] Questions and answers about time often involve idiomatic expressions, such as *Have you got the time?*; *What's the time?*; *Half-past*; *Just gone half eight*; *Quarter to*; *Nine on the dot*; *a few months back*; *two weeks ago*, etc. Familiar from ordinary talk, use of such expressions would wrench the narrative back into our present. In the texts explored here, distance from the here-and-now world was effectively achieved without undue threat to comprehensibility by careful management of how characters talk about time. Elric does not ask *What time is it?*; rather, he asks 'What's the hour'? (263); Shaarilla does not say *I have sought you for about three weeks now*, but 'I have sought you twenty days' (*Elric* 37); Moonglum does not say *It's almost morning*, but 'Dawn will be with us soon' (*Elric* 133); Easgathair White Owl does not announce *It's time*, but 'The appointed hour approaches' (*Lady* 543). Such references to time, often non-essential to the larger aspects of the plot and easy to miss, nevertheless play an important role in maintaining the stability of the past constructed in the text without losing the reader.

Consider as well that the archaic and intermediate styles are not varied randomly, but tend instead to be used together to good effect, as illustrated in the following passage from *Elric*.

Within the room something invisible and intangible – but sensed all the same – flowed and hovered over the sprawled body of Theleb K'aarna. Elric looked out of the window and thought he heard the beating of dragon wings – smelled the acrid breath of dragons – saw a shape winging across the dawn sky bearing Dyvim Tvar the Dragon Master away.

Elric half-smiled. 'The Gods of Melniboné protect *thee* wherever *thou* art,' he said quietly and turned away from the carnage, leaving the room.

On the stairway, he met Nikorn of Ilmar.

The merchant's rugged face was full of anger. He trembled with rage. There was a big sword in his hand.

'So I've found you, wolf,' he said. 'I gave you your life – and you have done this to me!' (*Elric* 114, italics mine)

Here, the intermediate style is used with the archaic style. In addition, the two used together suggest not only a past world, but a past world with a past of its own. In talk with mortal human characters, Elric uses the intermediate style, the language of his present (*you have done this to me*). When he addresses supernatural beings, he uses the language of his ancestors, 'the alien words of his forefathers' (9). The shift to Elric's own distant past is marked in the style by the shift from the intermediate to the archaic (*thee* and *thou*).

This chapter has demonstrated that alternative world texts often make skilled use of archaic forms in order to plausibly represent settings in the distant past. This involves a degree of complexity for which these texts seldom receive credit. When the alternative world is a past world, the use of archaic forms can be a significant aspect of style. Characters are often presented as members of earlier speech communities not only through their use of archaic words and grammatical structures, but also through their use of archaic speech acts. As also demonstrated in this chapter, the use of archaic forms in alternative world texts is a carefully controlled distortion. Syntactic deviations challenge the reader without impairing comprehension entirely, and the archaic style is rarely the only style in the text.

Chapter 4

Extraordinary Worlds in Plain Language

In the two preceding chapters, one of the primary concerns was to challenge the widely held view that alternative world texts tend to avoid experiments in form. Chapter 2 looked at innovative representations of language contact, and Chapter 3 investigated the stylistic opportunities opened up by the use of the archaic style. As Stockwell (2000: 73) points out, this kind of work is, in one sense, relatively easy, since it involves looking at language that is purposefully made to be noticed. Here in this chapter, the focus is on language that is not particularly noticeable, at least not to the untrained eye, and the point is to show that even this so called 'plain' or 'pedestrian' language is nevertheless working to achieve a number of literary effects.

That plain language in alternative world texts can still be effective language should come as no surprise. After all, as fantasy writer/critic Lin Carter (1973: 83) points out, authors such as Ernest Hemingway and Raymond Chandler made their name with plain language and are celebrated. Plain language in realist literature, to borrow a phrase from Toolan (1988: 117), is called 'art that conceals art'. In alternative world fiction, however, it is seldom valued in this way. More often, it is ranked only just above writing that is manifestly bad (Stockwell 2000: 76), and tolerated only to the extent that it does not interfere with the story. The analyses undertaken here demonstrate that this view of style in alternative world texts may be in need of revision. As Delany (1976/1977: 212) notes, language, no matter how plain, is always up to something in fiction, be it science, realist or otherwise:

[t]he concept of a writer writing a vivid and accurate scene in a language transparent and devoid of decoration so that we see

through to the object without writerly distraction suffers from the same contradiction as the concept of a painter painting a vivid and accurate scene with pigments transparent and devoid of color – so that the paint will not get between us and the picture. (Delany 1976/1977: 212)

In a similar analogy, C. S. Lewis (1961) points out that appreciating fiction without considering technique is like appreciating a statue without considering its shape, an absurd position given that a statue is what it is by virtue of its shape (Lewis 1961: 84). Just as there can be no picture without paint, and no statue without shape, there can be no story without style. Drawing on such insights, largely but unjustly neglected in the study of alternative world fiction, I show here in this chapter that alternative world texts can do some very extraordinary things with seemingly ordinary language to present the incredible as already believed, and the as yet uncertain future as already upon us. The claim that plain language can be used to increase the believability of alternative world texts has, of course, already been made in a number of places (e.g. see Amis 1960: 118; Attebery 1992: 6; Irwin 1976: 80, 194; Stockwell 2000: 51; Timmerman 1983: 52). Too often, however, it is put forward as just another way of seeking to excuse writing that has already been accepted as poor without sufficient scrutiny (Delany 1969: 61). A considered look at the supposedly plain language of alternative world texts reveals that it does not need excusing, but appreciating.

As noted in Chapter 1, it is frequently said that alternative world texts must 'somehow' put the impossible across as believable (Parker 1956: 598), make the 'non-fact appear as fact' (Irwin 1976: 9), and render the fantastic 'mundane' (Roberts 2001: 21). The alternative world constructed in the narrative must compel belief, at least as long as readers are reading (Stockwell 2000: 12; Tolkien 1947/1964: 36). A futuristic world must be 'reasonable and coherent' (Stockwell 2000: 12), and a magical world, while free, perhaps, from the laws of physics, must nevertheless follow the rules of its own proposing (Tolkien 1947/1964: 36; Le Guin 1979/1993). The successful 'story-maker', says Tolkien (1947/1964)

makes a Secondary World which your mind can enter. Inside it, what he relates is 'true': it accords with the laws of that world.

You therefore believe it, while you are, as it were, inside. (Tolkien 1947/1964: 36)

Writers of modern alternative world texts have in this respect a harder job than their counterparts in medieval romance (Lewis 1961: 62; Manlove 1975: 258; Shippey 1977: 149; Swinfen 1984: 2–3). As Swinfen (1984) puts it,

> the literal-mindedness of the modern reader militates against the writer of fantasy. With their wider interpretation of what could, or might, constitute human experience, earlier audiences were readier to accept a Grendel or a Green Man. The modern writer must expend much effort in order to induce 'secondary belief'. (Swinfen 1984: 2–3)

While it is widely appreciated that alternative world texts must take special care where plausibility is concerned, less frequently appreciated is the way that language can work to lend credibility. Tolkien (1947/1964) noted that the fantastic had to be 'presented as true' (19), and what he suggested for secondary world fantasies applies to alternative world fiction more generally. They

> cannot tolerate any frame or machinery suggesting that the whole story in which they occur is a figment or illusion. (Tolkien 1947/1964: 19)

This would admit disbelief, and

> the moment disbelief arises, the spell is broken; the magic, or rather the art, has failed. You are then out in the Primary World again, looking at the little abortive secondary world from outside. (Tolkien 1947/1964: 36)

The spell breakers Tolkien (1947/1964) mentions, however, such as characters waking from a dream at the end of the story, are more about content than style. Following Tolkien (1947/1964), both Timmerman (1983) and Irwin (1976) notice the impossible presented as true in a number of texts. Neither of them, however, is able to account in a detailed way for how this illusion might work. Irwin (1976), for example, tends instead to describe the result:

> [T]he opening situation has the external signs of an ensuing narrative, until it becomes evident, without any departure from the sober tone of the presentation, that the situation is fantastic; (Irwin 1976: 68)

or,

> [T]he reader simply finds himself in A.D. 1995 or 39000 or the Stone Age or in New Crete; (Irwin 1976: 69)

and so on. In similar terms, Timmerman (1983: 53) asserts that authors 'assume a world, and then proceed to describe it'. Lewis (1961) comes closer with what he calls 'Realism of Presentation' (57),

> the art of bringing something close to us, making it palpable and vivid, by sharply observed or sharply imagined detail. (Lewis 1961: 57)

Like Ellison (cited in Delany 1969: 64), however, he mostly means 'the casually dropped-in reference'. But what makes such references come across as casual? What is it about the presentation of the detail that suggests reality?

Closer scrutiny reveals that presenting an unknown and unreal world as actual and taken for granted largely comes down to subtle manipulations of style. Consider, for example, the opening paragraphs of the chapter 'Bran' in George R. R. Martin's *A Game of Thrones* (Book One of *A Song of Ice and Fire*). In this passage, a young noble boy, Bran, goes with his brothers and various other nobles to see his father behead a man for the crime of desertion.

> The morning had dawned clear and cold, with a crispness that hinted at the end of summer. They set forth at daybreak to see a man beheaded, twenty in all, and Bran rode among them, nervous with excitement. This was the first time he had been deemed old

enough to go with his lord father and his brothers to see the king's justice done. It was the ninth year of summer, and the seventh of Bran's life.

The man had been taken outside a small holdfast in the hills. Robb thought he was a wildling, his sword sworn to Mance Rayder, the King-beyond-the-Wall. It made Bran's skin prickle to think of it. He remembered the hearth tales Old Nan told them. The wildlings were cruel men, she said, slavers and slayers and thieves. They consorted with giants and ghouls, stole girl children in the dead of night, and drank blood from polished horns. And their women lay with the Others in the Long Night to sire terrible half-human children.

But the man they found bound hand and foot to the holdfast wall awaiting the king's justice was old and scrawny, not much taller than Robb. He had lost both ears and a finger to frostbite, and he dressed all in black, the same as a brother of the Night's Watch, except that his furs were ragged and greasy. (Martin 1996: 13–14)

Elements of Bran's world that either do not (e.g. *the Night's Watch*) or cannot (e.g. *nine years of summer*) exist in ours are nevertheless assumed to exist and presented as utterly familiar. How does this happen? To a large extent, this is achieved by the deictic use of definite noun phrases. To explain how this works, a brief account of *deixis* and *noun phrases* will be helpful at this point. Deictic expressions include adverbs such as *here* and *there*, temporal expressions such as *now* and *then*, demonstratives such as *this* and *that*, and pronouns such as *you* and *I*. In order to fully understand such expressions, the hearer must know who the speaker is, and in what context (time, place, etc.) his or her utterance was made (Herman 1995: 26; Levinson 1983: 54). When we use deictic expressions as speakers, we are assuming that our hearers already know something of what we are talking about. In the utterance *I'll do that*, for example, the *I* speaking is assuming that his or her hearer already knows, or will understand without explanation, what *that* refers to.

A noun phrase in English is, typically, a structure 'built up around a single noun' (Trask 1999: 207), such as *the white table* or *the new bicycle in the corner*. Grammars of English typically describe noun phrases as having four slots, one of which, the slot for the head noun, must always be filled. The other slots can be filled, but might not be. In the noun phrase *the big black car with tinted windows*, all the slots are filled. There is a determiner (*the*), premodification (*big, black*), a head noun (*car*), and postmodification (*with tinted windows*). Sometimes, noun phrases consist simply of single pronouns standing in for head nouns, such as *they* or *she* (Trask 1999: 207). Unmodified noun phrases, as the name suggests, are noun phrases without modification, either before or after the head noun. If we remove *big, black*, and *with tinted windows* from the example above, we are left with simply *the car*, an unmodified noun phrase.

The car is a definite noun phrase, as it contains the definite article *the*. The definite article *the* in English contrasts with the indefinite article *a/an*. The former introduces nouns that refer to concepts or things already known to both speaker and hearer, while the latter signals new, previously unknown information (Greenbaum and Quirk 1990: 77, 79–80). If, for example, I said 'I didn't get a wink of sleep of last night. *The* dog kept barking,' I am introducing this particular dog as one already familiar to both myself as speaker and my interlocutor as hearer. If I use *a* instead of *the*, however, the implication changes: 'I didn't get a wink of sleep last night. *A* dog kept barking.' Here, *dog* is introduced as new information, something the speaker assumes is not yet known to the hearer.

Definite noun phrases can be used deictically (Traugott 1981: 120; Traugott and Pratt 1980: 280–1), since a full understanding of what they refer to requires that the speaker and hearer share, at least in part, a common frame of reference. As Traugott and Pratt (1980: 280) explain, the use of *the* encodes the speaker's assumption that the hearer will have prior knowledge of, or immediately recognize, the thing that he or she mentions. Applying this to fictional discourse, narrators who introduce people or places or things with *the* are assuming that readers already know about them (Traugott 1981: 119–20; Wright and Hope 1996: 21–2). Alternative world texts often use definite noun phrases deictically to introduce imaginary or impossible features of their other worlds as though they were accepted givens (for a cognitive account of how these and other 'plain' elements work in alternative world texts, see Stockwell 2000: Chapters 2 and 7). In this way, readers are cast, linguistically at least, as already believing the incredible. In the passage cited above from *A Game of Thrones*, for example, *the king's justice, the ninth year of summer, the King-beyond-the-Wall, the Others, the Long Night* and *the Night's Watch* all refer to imagined elements particular to the created world of which Bran is a part. They represent some of the cardinal points of difference between our world and Bran's, and yet they are presented as already known through the device of the deictic noun phrase.

Reinforcing this illusion is the use of only slight modification. The noun phrases cited are not only definite, but relatively bare. Had explanatory information been embedded in pre- or postmodification, the illusion of familiarity would have been compromised. Contrast, for example, *the Night's Watch*, with *the Night's Watch, a once respected defence force in Bran's world now fallen on hard times*. The concentration of proper nouns also heightens the effect, representing significant cultural institutions as taken-for-granted givens. In the same way that many realist novels would not stop to explain Christmas or Kleenex, neither does *A Game of Thrones* stop to explain *the Long Night* or *The Others*. In a few short paragraphs, the humble noun phrase actualizes an entirely imagined culture with its own climate, institutions, enemies and beliefs.

Definite noun phrases are used in a similar way in the opening chapter of Robin Hobb's *Assassin's Apprentice* (Book One of *The Farseer Trilogy*). As the novel begins, the protagonist Fitz is attempting to write a history of his homeland. To us, this homeland is a magical otherworld unknown on Earth, but it is introduced simply as 'the six Duchies' (Hobb 1996: 1). Other new and significant references to the geo-politics of Fitz's world are also presented as already known: 'the first Duchy'; 'the Sea'; 'the Outislands' (1).

Fitz happens to have a compulsive form of telepathy, and this unreal ability is also introduced for the first time as a known and familiar phenomenon in the definite noun phrase 'the Skill' (2).

Or could the completeness of the memory be the bright overlay of the Skill, and the later drugs a man takes to control his addiction to it, the drugs that bring on pains and cravings of their own? (2–3)

Notice as well that it is not the information new to the reader, the Skill, that is the focus here, but the memory. The Skill is mentioned as just one of various things that might account for it, and further de-emphasized by an almost immediate shift to another topic, the drugs. Once again, it is noun phrases that are instrumental in achieving this effect. The Skill, revealed in an unmodified definite noun phrase, is presented as given, and thus dealt with swiftly. The drugs, in contrast, are presented as new, introduced in two successive and heavily modified noun phrases that arrest our attention ('the *later* drugs *a man takes to control his addiction to it*'; 'the drugs *that bring on pains and cravings of their own*').

Fitz also has the ability to communicate telepathically with animals, and this is introduced to us in the same way that Fitz himself considers it – as completely normal.

> I remember that first night well, the warmth of the hounds, the prickling straw, and even the sleep that finally came as the pup cuddled close beside me. I drifted into his mind and shared his dim dreams of an endless chase, pursuing a quarry I never saw, but whose hot scent dragged me onward through nettle, bramble, and scree. (Hobb 1996: 14)

Here, noun phrases introduce a string of memories consisting of elements familiar to both the reader's world and to Fitz's: 'the warmth', 'the hounds', 'the prickling straw', 'the sleep that finally came', 'the pup'. Placed right at the end of the sequence of normality is the extraordinary: drifting into the dog's mind and sharing a dream. The shift to the extraordinary is not linguistically marked. The first person narration continues without pause, as does the use of the simple past ('drifted', 'shared'). The key vocabulary items in the shared dream, such as 'scent', 'chase', 'quarry', 'nettle', and 'bramble' are lexically coherent with those in Fitz's own memory: 'hounds', 'pup', 'prickling' and 'straw.' Far from just ordinary and in no need of excusing, the ordinary language here is strategically effective in its own right.

The short story 'Amen and Out' by Brian Aldiss (first published in 1966, all citations and references from the 1983 reprint in *New Arrivals, Old Encounters*) also demonstrates how supposedly plain language can be effectively used to depict the new and unexpected as commonplace. Accounts of 'Amen and Out', few and brief to begin with, do not emphasize issues of style. Griffin and Wingrove (1984), for example, focus on matters of content and the ways in which 'Amen and Out' fits with Aldiss's wider body of work. While such aspects are illuminating and worthy of study, style is not an issue to be skipped in this story. Definite noun phrases are once again instrumental, as are adverbials. Adverbials are clause elements (along with, for example, subjects, verbs, and objects), that add information to a clause, often concerning matters of location, time, manner, or emphasis. Adverbials are varied in form, and can consist of prepositional phrases (They travelled *by train*), noun phrases (They walked *a long way*), adverb phrases (*Certainly* I'll come), and clauses, either finite (with tense, as in We stayed in *because it rained*), non-finite (without tense, for example, *Standing there on the platform*, she made her decision), or verbless (*When in Rome*, do as the Romans) (Greenbaum and Quirk 1990: 158, 161). Adverbials are often optional elements, and can be removed without impairing the syntactic structure of the sentence.

In the opening pages of 'Amen and Out', definite noun phrases (in italics in the examples below) and adverbials (underlined) introduce a number of mysterious futuristic details as though they were ordinary, even dull. There are shrines of some sort, associated in some way with lights and altars:

> He tucked his feet into slippers and went over to *the shrine by the window,* (56)
> The curtains that normally concealed *the shrine* slid back; (57)
> He did not approach *the shrine in his small room*; (57)
> *the unlit shrine,* (57)
> *the light* came on behind *the altar,* (59)
> *The light* failed to glow behind *the altar.* (60)

changes in lifestyle:

> These Immortals are our brains. Frankly, <u>in this star-going age</u>, we can't afford to be without them; (65)

> Although, as a human, he played a not unimportant role in the city,
>   it was primarily a city of machines; (56–7)

and a project of some kind, involving something called a wethouse
and beings known as Immortals:

> I will spend the day working at *the project*; (56)
> the walls of *the project* gleamed brightly; (57)
> I notice you've still got your mouldy ill-paid job as doorman *at the
>   project!*; (58)
> Inside, *Darkling's immortals* were imprisoned; (57)
> the housing and guarding of *the Immortals* was his responsibility; (61)
> Despite his two hundred years and his zebra-striped effect, Palmer
>   looked younger than the shaggy, whiskery Otto; (66)
> They walked together into the antechamber of *the Wethouse*, pulling
>   on boots and oilskins; (61)
> As he walked through to *the first Wethouse* he saw with some
>   disapproval that young Zee Stone was on duty and flirting with
>   a slight blonde secretary. (61)

Neither the narrator nor the characters stop to explain any of these
things at the beginning of the story, because they are meant to come
across as pre-existing familiar elements in a known world. The definite noun phrases encode them as recognizable or previously known,
and the adverbials de-emphasize them as background information.
Interstellar travel, second-class status to machines, and the Immortality Investigation Project (an organization that exploits people who
have acquired an indefinite lifespan) are all introduced in an off-hand
way as subsidiary to something else by their placement in optional
and syntactically dependent adverbials. Take, for instance, the final
example listed above, repeated here for convenience:

> As he walked through to *the first Wethouse* he saw with some disap-
> proval that young Zee Stone was on duty and flirting with a slight
> blonde secretary. (61)

Here, the main business of the clause in terms of the syntax is Zee
Stone's flirting and his boss's disapproval. The Wethouse, a special

chamber in the project for housing the imprisoned Immortals, is tucked away in an optional adverbial.

In 'Amen and Out', the ordinary language that introduces these strange things as familiar gradually allows them to actually become so without corpsing the illusion that the future has already come to pass. This can be illustrated with the shrines, the nature of which becomes increasingly clear as the story progresses. A series of ordinary noun phrases referring to the shrines provides clues to their use while at the same time suggesting mundane experience for the characters.

the bedside shrine; (58–9)
the shrine on his back; (59)
his pocket shrine; (65)
his old second-hand shrine; (69)
the portable shrine. (60)

Ordinary verb phrases (italicized below) provide further clues. We are told, for example, that the character Otto

snapped open his portable shrine; (60)
unstrapped his old second-hand shrine; (69)
set it *up* before him; (69)
opened it; (69)
struck it when the altar light refused to glow. (69)

Like the noun phrases, these verb phrases suggest habitual and routine activity for the characters, while at the same time sketching in an increasingly complete picture of the shrines for the reader. A very telling clue is delivered in one of Otto's answered prayers:

And buy a new battery for this altar. (60)

There is nothing ornate or very noticeable in the prose here. The instruction is a simple sentence consisting of one clause in the expected imperative mood. It is this very simplicity, however, that delivers the effect. In an unremarkable piece of dialogue ostensibly about something else (Otto's arrogant irreverence towards his gods), we find out that shrines are battery-operated.

The picture that emerges from these plain language clues eventually becomes very recognizable. The shrines are portable, come in table-top, laptop and pocket varieties, light up when you snap them open, can be bought new or second-hand, get a frustrated thwack when they do not work properly, and run on batteries. Published in 1966, 'Amen and Out' predicts an age when the personal computer – desktops, laptops, palm-tops, the lot – becomes just one more appliance, like the refrigerator or the washing machine. Ordinary language sustains the illusion that this future had already come to pass at the time the story was written.

Ordinary expressions of tense and aspect, so ordinary, in fact, that they are easy to miss, are another means by which fantastic elements and events are normalized in alternative world texts.[1] In Tad Williams' *Otherland* (also discussed in Chapter 2, pages 47–57), for example, events that have not and may never occur, people routinely dying in neurologically induced virtual reality simulations, are related in the past tense (italicized in passage below) as already old news in the speech of the character Renie:

'A decade or so ago you *used to* hear about a netboy or netgirl dying every couple of weeks – too long under simulation, *forgot* they *needed* real food and real water. Not to mention ordinary things like pressure sores. Doesn't happen much anymore – too many safeguards on the commercial products, too many restrictions and alarm routines on net access at universities and in business'. (V1: 39)

The switch to the present (in *doesn't*) introduces what are from our perspective circumstances even further in the future (people getting used to the technology and not dying), but presents them as current realities for the speaker. Seemingly ordinary language organizes a series of what-ifs and maybes pertaining to our near and not so near future into a logically consistent then-but-not now narrative structure, lending the speculations the semblance of reality.

Contrasts between the simple past (*he walked*) and the past per-
fective (*he had walked*) play a similar role in the opening of Aldiss's
'Three Ways' (1978, citations from the reprint in *New Arrivals, Old
Encounters*, 1983). (Story also discussed in Chapter 5, pages 138–40).

> The *Bathycosmos* was all but home. It lay in the shallow of space [. . .]
> Little police flitters, media craft, supply torpedoes [. . .] approached
> the gigantic research vessel [. . .] They drifted across the great cliff
> of hull [. . .]
>   [. . .] The photographers and spectrum analysts had been roused,
> from cryogenic sleep. They had undergone the rituals of exercise
> and dance, and had taken the first semi-liquid meal. Digestion
> began again, after many Earth years. They were feeling more like
> human beings, less like revenants. (27, ellipses mine)

The passage begins in the past tense (*was, lay, approached, drifted*)
which, as Wright and Hope (1996: 50) point out, is the normal and
expected tense in fictional narratives. Typically, the use of the past
tense in fiction is interpreted as 'an implicit present' (Wright and
Hope 1996: 50), and the events described are read is if they are currently happening (Wright and Hope 1996: 55). Also normal in the
passage above is the switch to the past perfective (the photographers
and spectrum analysts *had been roused, had undergone, had taken*) to
relate background material, events posited as taking place before the
Bathycosmos docked. All of the events described, however, are fantastic
and futuristic. Embedding them in an ordinary and consistent narrative tense structure allows them to be depicted as occurring in a logical
sequence. Alternative world texts such as *Otherland* and 'Amen and
Out' present the impossible by situating the as yet uncertain future
as the narrator's now. As Wright and Hope (1996: 54) point out, however, what matters in terms of plausibility is the internal consistency
of the time shifts in the narrative itself. The absolute relationship
between the narrator's now and the reader's is less important than the
relative relationship between the narrator's now and the events that
unfold from it. The narrator's now can be the same as the reader's, or
not. It can be the remote past, the distant future, or some magical

point outside time. It can be whenever, so long as the events and states narrated in the story can be logically related to it. Ordinary shifts in tense and aspect are what make that logic apparent.

Another important factor in the plausibility of alternative world texts, as Lewis (1961: 66) has observed, is the way in which characters react or are reported to react in or to fantastic events and settings. Hamlet's behaviour when he faces the ghost of the old king, suggests Lewis (1961: 66), is not presented to tell us more about him or, by extension, human nature, but to lend credence to the ghost. The much criticized 'plain' language of alternative world texts has an important role to play in this process, as well, as can be demonstrated in John Wyndham's *Chocky* (1968). Chocky, an alien intelligence, seeks to advise humanity, but can only communicate through a telepathic link to a young boy, Matthew. In the passage below, Chocky speaks through Matthew to Matthew's father.

> I want to talk to you because I shall not come back again after this. You will be glad to hear this: the other part of his parent, I mean mummy, I mean your wife, will be gladder because it is afraid of me and thinks I am bad for Matthew, which is a pity because I did not mean me, I mean you, I mean Matthew, any harm. Do you understand? (Wyndham 1968: 139)

In this passage, the fantastic experiences of telepathy and alien communication are given actuality as Chocky stumbles through her message. The stumbling does not tell us anything about Chocky in particular. It does not, for example, indicate that she is inarticulate or unintelligent or nervous. Neither is Chocky's stumbling representative of some wider message about communication in general. Rather, Chocky's stumbling suggests what it might actually be like to communicate through a telepathic mediator. The fact that she stumbles on certain specific noun phrases is no mere coincidence, but a significant feature of style. In ordinary speech situations, speakers and hearers take into account their differing perspectives. If, for example, two people – let us call them Jack and Jill – were talking about Jill's father, Jack would refer to him not as 'my father' or 'the father' or 'his father', but 'your father', and Jill would understand that he was referring to *her* father with this phrase rather than his own. It is precisely on this point of perspective that Chocky experiences difficulty during her mediated communication. Accustomed to communicating telepathically with Matthew, she has to first disentangle her perspective from his, and then take into account his father's when speaking to him through Matthew. Thus, Matthew's mother is first 'the other part of his parent' (Chocky's perspective), then 'Mummy' (Matthew's perspective), and finally 'your wife' (his father's perspective). Even more telling is her difficulty in talking about Matthew in the third person. In her first attempt, she equates Matthew with herself ('I did not mean *me* . . . any harm'). She then speaks as if addressing Matthew directly ('I did not mean *you* . . . any harm'), and only on her third try does she get it right ('I did not mean . . . *Matthew* any harm'). Chocky's references to Matthew's mother also indicate that gender is viewed very differently on her world. The noun phrase 'the other half of his parent', for example, suggests that among Chocky's people gender, or gender differences, may be either non-existent or irrelevant. In *Chocky*, a lived experience of telepathy and a radically different attitude to gender are suggested in a handful of ordinary noun phrases.[2]

Other examples of seemingly ordinary language indicating altered perspectives at a stroke are not difficult to find. In Stephen Baxter's *Conqueror* (2007), for example, Haley's Comet is for the Anglo-Saxon characters either just 'the comet' or 'the hairy star' (7); in *The Beautiful Journey* (2009), survivors of an environmental holocaust refer to glaciers and icebergs as 'wild ice'; in 'Amen and Out', the Christian Bible is 'the pre-Gods book' (60). In Gibson's *Neuromancer*, as Stockwell (2000) suggests, an altered world view is established in the opening line: 'The sky above the port was the color of television, tuned to a dead channel' (Gibson 1984: 9). This seemingly plain piece of language contains a subtle and effective inverted metaphor, as Stockwell (2000: 201–2) demonstrates. Metaphors typically work by inviting us to interpret an unfamiliar item in terms of a more familiar or more basic one. Stockwell (2000) argues that generally speaking, we would expect 'the sky' to be the more basic term, and other things to be interpreted in light of it (e.g. 'sky blue'). In *Neuromancer*, however, it is the sky that is treated as unfamiliar and explained in terms of the television screen, not the other way round, suggesting a future where one of the given 'cultural assumptions' (Stockwell 2000: 201) is that 'televisions are more basic and natural than the sky' (202).

The presentation of the impossible as actual can also be enhanced by engaging the reader's involvement. In a wider sense, potentially any narrative might exhibit this strategy, even a conversational one. As Brown and Levinson (1978/1987) note, speakers telling stories in conversation often spontaneously employ linguistic devices which make those stories more interesting or entertaining for their listeners. Such devices include exaggerations (*There were a million people in the queue ahead of me!*), use of the vivid present (*And then I say . . .*), rhetorical questions (*And wouldn't you know it?*) and other expressions that treat the listener as an active participant (e.g. the interjection *you know*). These devices serve to draw listeners 'right into the middle of events being discussed' (Brown and Levinson 1978/1987: 106).

Drawing readers into a story is, of course, the business of fiction, and a particular concern in alternative world fiction, as readers must be drawn into an entirely imagined and non-mimetic world. If this otherworld is sufficiently compelling, as Swinfen (1984) and Tolkien (1947/1964) have argued, readers may be less likely to say 'But dragons and trolls and androids can't really exist', and more likely to ask, 'But what will happen to the dragon and the troll and the android?' In alternative world texts, it is often ordinary – and ordinarily unnoticeable linguistic devices – that encourage this kind of involvement. Adverbials, for example, the optional clause elements introduced earlier, can play an important role in intensifying the emotional impact of a description or scene by delaying key information. They are used this way to remarkable effect in Dunsany's *The King of Elfland's Daughter* (also discussed in Chapter 3). Prince Alveric's journey to Elfland, for instance, is invested with excitement and anticipation nearly from start to finish, and this effect is largely due to the way adverbials are used. Alveric's first act is to commission an enchanted sword, and adverbial elements (numbered in the examples below), in delaying the ultimate appearance of the sword, heighten expectation:

And (1) flat in the glow, (2) all liquid still, lay the sword. (Dunsany 1924/1969: 6)

On the day of his actual departure, Alveric does not simply wake up; rather, he is, it is suggested in a series of delaying adverbials, sought out by the sun.

(1) To the long chamber, (2) sparsely furnished, (3) high in a tower, (4) in which Alveric slept, there came a ray direct from the rising sun. (Dunsany 1924/1969: 9)

When he sees the King of Elfland's palace after the long and dangerous journey, the moment is not just reported, but dramatized.

And (1) jutting from that wood, (2) with glittering portals all open wide to the lawns, (3) with windows more blue than our sky on summer's nights; (4) as though built of starlight; shone that palace that may be only be told of in song. (Dunsany 1924/1969: 20–1)

The glorious palace is presented only after a series of four delaying adverbial elements that heighten expectation. Alveric does not just come round the corner and see the castle. He encounters it. Arrested by its beauty, he stands before it spell-bound in awe, as do we – largely because of a series of adverbial elements.

Alveric has come to the palace for Lirazel, the King of Elfland's daughter who is to become his wife. His first glimpse of her is even more dramatically told:

(1) As Alveric stood there (2) with his sword in his hand, (3) at the wood's edge, (4) scarcely breathing, (5) with his eyes looking over the lawns at the chiefest glory of Elfland; (6) through one of the portals (7) alone came the King of Elfland's daughter. (Dunsany 1024/1969: 21)

No less than seven adverbials delay the arrival of the princess. This allows tension to build up, leaving us, like Alveric, nearly breathless with anticipation.

The King tries to prevent his daughter from leaving Elfland with Alveric, but is too late. Just as he is about to say the spell that 'would hold his daughter in Elfland forever' (Dunsany 1924/1969: 38), she leaves with Alveric, and a string of adverbials lead us to the King at this moment, intensifying for us the impact of his grief.

> And (1) standing there all blue and white against his silver tower, (2) aged by the passing of times of which we know nothing, (3) before he imposed its eternal calm upon Elfland, he thought of his daughter amongst our pitiless years. (Dunsany 1924/1939: 38)

The loading of adverbials in this way allows for attitudes and emotions to emerge organically from the experiences described, often a more effective way of fostering reader involvement than narrating emotional states at a distance (e.g. *The King grieved; the Prince felt excited*).

Adverbials in *The King of Elfland's Daughter* also dramatize major turning points in the plot. Alveric and Lirazel do wed and are happy for a time, but it does not last. When the King offers Lirazel a way back to Elfland, she eventually takes it, riding an enchanted wind back to her home. The moment of Lirazel's departure from Alveric's world ends the chapter, and the suspense hanging on this moment is further amplified by the adverbials that the delay the action:

> and (1) away with a riot of dancing and glory of colour, (2) high in the light of the sun that had set from the sight of the fields, went wind and leaves together. With them went Lirazel. (Dunsany 1924/ 1969: 63)

Upon Lirazel's return to Elfland, the King magically puts the kingdom beyond human interference by removing it from the mortal world. A series of adverbials, however, leads us through the enchanted peace of the kingdom to the troll Lurulu:

> And (1) there below motionless fronds of dream-gripped trees, (2) on the still water (3) dreaming of the still air, (4) where the huge lily-leaves floated green in the calm, was the troll Lurulu, sitting upon a leaf. (Dunsany 1924/1969: 104)

A troll sitting on a leaf may seem more curious than ominous. The delaying adverbials, however, increase the time it takes us to get to this information, heightening tension and creating suspense. It is this that invests Lurulu's eventual appearance here with such menace, and for good reason. As we are later to discover, Lurulu is something of a chink in the King's magical armour, as it is he who will breach the sealed border and bring Elfland back into contact with human kind.

As unlikely as it may seem, prepositional phrases, units of language that begin with a preposition (*on, in, under,* etc.) and are completed by a noun phrase (e.g. *in the house, over the moon, up the road*) can also intensify the emotional impact of a scene. An example of the way this works is found in the description of a place called Bingtown in Robin Hobb's *The Mad Ship* (1999, Book Two of *The Liveship Traders* trilogy).

Bingtown was cupped in a sparkling blue bay. Rolling hills in the bright greens of spring backed the lively merchant town. Even before they docked, she could smell the smoke and cooking and cattle. The shrill cries of the hawkers in the market floated out over the water. The streets bustled with traffic, and the waters of the harbour were no less busy. Small craft plied back and forth between the shore and anchored ships. Little fishing vessels threaded their way through the tall-masted merchant ships to bring their catch to market. It was a symphony of sight and sound and smell, and its name was Bingtown. (Hobb 1999: 189)

At first glance, the language does not seem to be up to very much here. Nothing jumps out at us stylistically or calls attention to itself. If we consider the passage without its prepositional phrases, however, what they contribute becomes immediately apparent.

Bingtown was cupped. Rolling hills backed the lively merchant town. They docked, she could smell the smoke and cooking and cattle. The shrill cries floated. The streets bustled, and the waters were no less busy. Small craft plied. Little fishing vessels threaded their way to bring their catch. It was a symphony, and its theme was Bingtown. (Hobb passage with prepositional phrases removed)

As Wright and Hope (1996) have noted, prepositional phrases accomplish far more in literary texts than they are typically given credit for.

Without the prepositional phrases, the description dissolves. A picture of sorts is painted, but not a very rich one. The passage is reduced to something more like a list, and it is difficult to see how its separate components fit together into a coherent scene. For example, is 'Bingtown' the same place as 'the lively merchant town'? The relationship of sameness between these two is not clear without the linking phrase 'in a sparkling blue bay'. The absence of this particular prepositional phrase also casts doubt on the action of docking. Where does the ship dock exactly? 'The lively merchant town', which may or may not be Bingtown, does not necessarily have to have a harbour. Reading further without the prepositional phrases leads to more questions. For instance, do the 'shrill cries' belong to the cattle or the bustling streets? What was a vivid and detailed scene has become an incoherent jumble.

The prepositional phrases would be significant from this angle alone, as richly detailed descriptions of places are an important feature of alternative world texts. The more fantastic the world, the more detailed its physical settings need to be (Hunt in Hunt and Lenz 2001/2004; Swinfen 1984; Thompson 1982). There is, however, more to it than this. Prepositional phrases, as Wright and Hope (1996: 155) note, also play an important 'orientating function.' In essence, they say 'Look – follow me – I have something to show you.' This has the effect of putting the reader in contact with what feels like 'a consciousness' (Wright and Hope 1996: 155). Without the prepositional phrases, this relationship between describer and reader is largely lost. A random sequence of events (the shrill cries floated, the streets bustled, etc.) does not imply any kind of thought or agency, and so is difficult to care about. A coherent scene, on the other hand, implies an emotional investment. Someone is looking out at the town, and cares about what they see. This makes it more likely that the reader will care, or at least wonder why the scene seems of such heightened importance.

The orientating consciousness in the passage belongs to Althea, who is returning after almost a year's absence and surveys her hometown from the deck of a ship. While the passage is narrated in the third person, the orientating prepositional phrases give it the 'subjective immediacy' (Wright and Hope 1996: 155) more usually associated with first person narration. This effect is enhanced by the delaying function that prepositional phrases can have (Wright and Hope 1996: 155). As she approaches Bingtown, Althea's level of emotion rises, and a corresponding tension builds in the prose as the prepositional phrases mount up in the scene. The final sentence has a particularly significant impact, and parallels Althea's 'sudden rush of emotion, stronger than any homesickness' (188), upon seeing Bingtown. Without the prepositional phrases, the final sentence is just one more random item on the list, equal in importance (or unimportance, as the case may be) to all of the other items. The fact that it occurs last could just be a coincidence. With the prepositional phrases there to delay its arrival and heighten expectation, the final sentence is, to carry on the symphony metaphor introduced in the passage itself, delivered in a dramatic crescendo with a clash of cymbals indicative of Althea's feelings.

Prepositional phrases work the same way in a passage a few pages later when Althea leaves the ship to visit her family home.

The Vestrit Mansion, like the homes of the other Bingtown Traders, was set in the cool and forested foothills that surrounded Bingtown itself. It was a brief carriage ride from the docks, or a comfortable walk on a pleasant day. Along the way, one could glimpse other elegant Trader homes set well back from the main road. She passed flowering hedges and drives lined with trees extravagantly green with spring growth. Ivy sprawled in a mantle over the Oswell's stone wall. Crisp yellow daffodils were showing their first blooms in clumps by their gate. The spring day was rich with birdcalls and the dappling shade of newly leafed tress and the scents of early flowers.

Never before had it seemed to be such a long walk. (Hobb 1999: 195)

Without the prepositional phrases, a coherent passage is once again reduced to a seemingly random list:

The Vestrit Mansion was set. It was a brief carriage ride, or a comfortable walk. One could glimpse other elegant Trader homes set well. She passed flowering hedges and drives lined. Ivy sprawled. Crisp yellow daffodils were showing their first blooms. The spring day was rich. Never had it seemed to be such a long walk.

The absence of the prepositional phrases leaves the basic outline mostly intact, but it seems of no importance to anyone, character or reader. With the prepositional phrases, a richly detailed and coherent scene comes alive and, once again, the implied consciousness at work behind the phrases acts as our guide, this time bringing us ever closer to the old Vestrit Mansion. And, as in the Bingtown passage, the prepositional phrases accomplish a delaying effect that increases the emotional impact of the final sentence. This is made all the more dramatic by the introduction of a sudden contrast. Many of the prepositional phrases carry positive details about the scene: *cool and forested, pleasant, extravagantly green, spring growth, bird calls, newly leafed trees*. These are at odds with the doom-tolling final sentence: 'Never before had it seemed to be such a long walk'. Althea is unsure of her welcome and nervous about her homecoming. The beauty of the scene as she draws closer to her home becomes a cruel insult to her inner turmoil.

Because prepositional phrases are subtle and often work below the level of conscious awareness, their importance is easy to miss. As the analysis above has shown, however, easy to miss does not mean insignificant. In *The Mad Ship*, prepositional phrases establish an orientating link with the reader, turning descriptions of place into dramatized reflections of character emotions.

In taking a closer look at 'plain' language in a number of alternative world texts, this chapter has shown that it is a great deal more than merely adequate. Simple definite noun phrases (and it does not get much plainer than that in English) evoke familiarity for the unknown, ordinary realizations of tense and aspect normalize fantastic events, unremarkable structures instantly establish altered perspectives, and mundane prepositional phrases and adverbials motivate reader involvement. Style in the alternative world texts studied here is not subordinated to ideas or mythic scope and is not in need of excusing; rather, it is an integral part of the narratives working to create in words other worlds that are physically, temporally, culturally and emotionally convincing. In the next chapter, the exploration of plain language in alternative world fiction continues as we turn to another much-maligned feature of these texts, the creation of character.

Chapter 5

Style and Character

The previous chapter demonstrated that 'plain' language in alternative world texts is nevertheless effective language, especially when it comes to actualizing an imaginary world. In this chapter, the role of supposedly plain language in presenting a convincing world is again the focus as we investigate style and character. As Toolan (1988: 90), Chatman (1978: 113) and Woolf (1924/1950) have all noted, it is the exploration of character that often makes fiction attractive to readers. In alternative world fiction, character is especially important, as readers are more likely to 'remain' in the alternative world, as it were, if they find there characters with which they can identify (Hunt, in Hunt and Lenz 2001/2004: 9; Schlobin 1982: ix; Stockwell 2000: 213). As I will demonstrate in this chapter, such characters are generally thought to be lacking in alternative world fiction, an assumption that has adversely affected their critical reception and evaluation. That convincing and compelling characters do populate the pages of alternative world fiction is clear, I suggest, when style is considered primary in the creation of character.

Accounts of character in fiction or drama (e.g. Chatman 1978; Culpeper 2001; Toolan 1988) generally concern themselves in one way or another with three questions: (1) whether or not characters can be said to exist; (2) whether or not it is appropriate to think of characters as being like people; and (3) which is to be considered primary in narrative, character or plot. The answers to questions one and two are relatively straightforward. 'Character', as Toolan (1988: 91) notes, 'is an illusion.' Characters in fiction do not exist as such, but 'are sets of traits attached to a name' (quote from Chatman 1978: 137, see also Attebery 1992: 72; Leech and Short 1981/2007: 297; Toolan 1988: 93). Readers, however, tend to evaluate and react to these 'illusions' and 'sets of traits' as though they were real people (Chatman 1978: 125; Culpeper 2001: 10; Leech and Short 1981/2007: 297; Stockwell 2003b: 258; Toolan 1988: 92; Woolf 1924/1950). The answer to question three is more complicated, at least with respect to the study of alternative world fiction. Broadly speaking, narratives can be character-driven or plot-driven (Chatman 1978: 113) and characters can be either represented people, or plot devices, roles or types (such as 'hero') with specific functions (save the kingdom). In the critical literature, alternative world texts are typically viewed as plot-driven narratives (e.g. see Brooke-Rose 1981: 248; Hume 1984: 150; Thompson 1982: 223) and their characters corresponding analysed mostly as types – the maverick (Amis 1960: 84); the worthy orphan (Sullivan 1996: 305–6); the hero (Manlove 1982: 31; Thompson 1982).

Both represented individuals and types are, as Attebery (1992: 72), Chatman (1978: 113), and Toolan (1988: 92) have pointed out, equally valid. Neither one is better or worse than the other, and preferences for one over the other that sometimes emerge tend to reflect the prevailing convention rather than judgements based on merit (Chatman 1978: 113). In discussions on alternative world fiction, however, the difference between character-as-type and character-as-individual is often interpreted in terms of deficit, with types being viewed negatively as 'flat' and realized individuals considered positively as 'round'. The distinction between 'flat' and 'round', originally set out by Forster (1927) in *Aspects of the Novel*, has, as Chatman (1978: 131) notes, stood the test of time and is compatible with trait theory (Chatman 1978: 131). Flat characters, which do not change or develop (Forster 1927/2000: 74) and are 'constructed round a single idea or quality' (Forster 1927/2000: 74), can be said to have few traits, while round characters, more complex and not reducible to a single idea (Forster 1927: 81), can be said to have a variety of traits (Chatman 1978: 132).

With only few exceptions[1] characters in alternative world texts are dismissed as flat and poorly drawn. In fantasy, it is said, characters 'are often thin' (Hume 1984: 123), 'superficial' (Brooke-Rose 1981: 248), nothing more than stock types (Brooke-Rose 1981: 248), so lacking in depth they 'could often go nameless' (Mobley 1973: 127).

Only 'very rarely', asserts Attebery (1992: 70) do characters in fantasy 'resemble the sort of beings found in Ibsen's plays or nineteenth-century social novels'. As Meyers (1980: 128) and Scholes (1975: 47–8) have noted, science fiction has received the same sort of criticism with respect to character. Characters in pulp science fiction 'tend to be interchangeable' (Stockwell 2003b: 262) and exist only to explain the science (Attebery 1992, 2003: 33). In hard science fiction, a sub-genre grounded in technology and the physical sciences (Cramer 2003: 187), there are 'few if any psychologised characters' (Stockwell 2003b: 254). For Roberts (2006: 12), 'detailed and subtle analyses of character, or psychologised analyses' are hard to find, a point also made by Sanders (1979) and Russ (1975). 'The protagonists of science fiction are always collective, never individual persons', says Russ (1975: 113), and individuals that do occur are just types (113). In much the same terms as Attebery (1992) did for fantasy, Sanders (1979) writes off character and characterization in science fiction almost entirely: 'One is hard put to name half a dozen memorable characters in all the annals of the genre, to recall any science-fiction protagonist who hangs in the mind with the weight of Rashkolnikov, say, or Stephen Dedalus or Quentin Compson' (Sanders 1979: 131).

In many ways, the study of character in the literature on alternative world texts has paralleled the study of style. Its poverty is asserted, excuses for that poverty are put forward, and examples contrary to the initial assertion are waved away. What Sanders (1979) has noted about the treatment of character in science fiction, for example, applies equally well to fantasy: 'even sympathetic commentators concede [the] point' (131). Rather than question the initial judgement on character, many alternative world text scholars just accept it and then seek to explain or justify it, filling the critical record with apologist positions on the issue of character rather than in-depth and revealing studies. Yes, character is generally poor, such commentators say, but that need not be a concern because it is the ideas that are the heroes (Amis 1960; Broderick 2003: 51; Hume 1984: Mathews 1977: 18; 123; Parrinder 1979b: 155; Rose 1981: 30; Russ 1975: 116; Scholes 1975; Suvin 1972), or character universals such as 'loyalty' and 'courage' that matter (Attebery 1992: 109; Brooke-Rose 1981: 248; Parker 1956: 607; Thompson 1982: 223), or the mythic element, the soul-feeding story, that counts, particularly in fantasy (Attebery 1992: 54, 71, 85–6; Lewis 1961: 44; Mobley 1973: 126–7).

While Sanders (1979) complains about apologist positions offered by others, he goes on to present one himself. He accepts that characterization is typically poor in science fiction but claims this is because *'science fiction as a genre is centrally about the disappearance of character'* (Sanders 1979: 132, italics his). It subordinates character, he says, because it reflects society's fear that the autonomous self is under threat from the corrosive systems of the modern industrialized world (Sanders 1979). Roberts (2006: 113) and Stockwell (2003b) draw on reader-oriented frameworks (Marxist reification and schema theory, respectively) to account for their accepted stances on the poverty of characterization. Yes, characters do tend to be poorly drawn in science fiction, they are willing to admit, but that is not a problem because readers infer rich characterization even from very sparse textual details. Attebery (1992: 73), employing a similar strategy, invokes the notion of metafiction. Yes, we do encounter poor characterization in fantasy, he says, but that is only because it seeks to 'examine the relationship between character as imitated person and character as story function' (73), and thus 'calls into question the continuity of traits by which the reader is accustomed to identify characters' (73).[2] Sometimes, characterization is brushed aside altogether by supposing that a work is valuable for what it tells us about 'widespread cultural values and assumptions', an argument that Attebery (1992: 9) puts forward for the entire sub-genre of sword and sorcery.

When examples running counter to the characterization-is-poor thesis are found, they tend to be explained away. Numerous commentators, for example, note that alternative world texts do present human-like and 'psychologically valid' (Schlobin 1982: ix) characters, but then account for them as devices. They are '"realistic" focalisers' (Hunt 2001: 9), 'mediator[s]' (Shippey 1982: 55), 'emblematic counterparts' (Stockwell 2003b: 264) or 'bridge[s]' (Parker 1956: 599) that we use simply to cross from the world of the real to the alternative world of the text. According to Cramer (2003: 190), the convincing characters in Greg Bear's 'Tangents' (1986) and Vernor Vinge's 'Bookworm, Run!' (1966) do not convince because they are well drawn, but because parts of the plot, such as multi-dimensional travel and technological augmentation, lend them substance. Delany 1968/1977: 194) observes richly drawn characters in stories of the near future by authors such as Leiber, Merril, Pohl and Knight, but dismisses this as accidental. They convince because

> their social and psychological matrices are close enough to ours so that character insights and a sense of economic reality lend density and intensity much the same way they will to a mainstream story. (Delany 1968/1977: 194)

What is more troubling is that such examples may not be explained at all. Attebery (1992: 54), for example, accepts the 'character-as-type' judgement, and points specifically to Tolkien's characters as instances of types ('the wizard, the lady, the comic servant'). And yet, he himself seems to have found at least some of these characters convincing.

> Hidden within Gandalf the wise Old Man, the archetypal guide and protector, is a realistically depicted, irascible old tutor – undoubtedly a blend of characters met by Tolkien in real life, including himself in the role of educator. (Attebery 1992: 30)

Russ (1975) boldly asserts that science fiction is not interested in characterization, a position, according to her, that 'needs no citation' (113). She goes on to broadly dismiss the characters in Hal Clement's *Close to Critical* as 'neither interesting, probable, nor necessary' (116). Of the same author, however, she later claims with equal certainly that 'his characters are always rational, humane, and highly likeable' (116). Hume's (1984) account betrays a similar dissonance over the issue of characterization. Her starting position is that alternative world fiction 'based on character is relatively rare and exceedingly difficult to sustain' (Hume 1984: 161), and she cites, as one of the rare exceptions, Le Guin's *The Dispossessed.* However, she then carries on citing exceptions. Orwell's *Nineteen Eighty-four* is also a good character-based piece of alternative world fiction. As is Zamyatin's *We.* Oh, and so is Golding's *The Inheritors.* If it is so easy to find exceptions, is the initial point about 'rare and exceedingly difficult' valid? Hume

(1984) does not consider this, but instead dismisses the importance of the increasingly numerous exceptions by doggedly repeating her earlier point: alternative world texts based on character are 'difficult to create and sustain' (161).

A number of commentators blame the realist approach to literature and criticism, and call for different standards and criteria to be developed (e.g. Attebery 1992; de Camp 1976: 164; Parrinder 1979; Roberts 2006; Russ 1975). Parrinder (1979b), for example, says that frameworks predicated on notions such as autonomy and 'liberal individualism' (160) are not appropriately applied to characters in science fiction. Shippey (1982: 185) suggests that character in contemporary fantasy is not best judged by modern standards, since the genre is rooted in an older narrative tradition that did not psychologize its characters in ways familiar to us today.

The problem, however, may not be the characters in the texts or the way in which the notion of character is theorized. The problem may instead be one of method. That is, what seems to need attention is the way critics and analysts look for evidence about characters in alternative world texts. Typically, as Chatman (1978: 134) notes, this is a matter of considering what characters do, what they say, what is said to them, and what is said about them. In many literary-critical accounts of character the focus is on the actions characters do or do not take, or the semantic content of their speech and thought (what they talk and think about). As Culpeper (2001) reminds us, however, the illusion of character is created through language. Readers encounter words on the page, and characters come to life (Culpeper 2001: 1; Toolan 1988: 91). Close linguistic attention to these words in alternative world fiction can yield fresh insights about the creation of character in these texts. Consider, for example, four hypothetical story openings proposed by Delany (1969: 54):

> I put some things on the desk.
> I put some books on the desk.
> I put three books on the desk.
> I put Hacker's *The Terrible Children*, Ebbe Borregaard's *Collected Poems*, an Wakoski's *Inside the Blood Factory* on the Desk. (Delany 1969: 54)

As with the other examples of supposedly plain language discussed in Chapter 4, there does not seem much to notice here. There is no deviant syntax, no dialect variation, no created words, nothing unusual. All we have are four increasingly specific accounts of a particular action. As Delany (1969) points out, however, it is precisely this specificity that needs to be noticed.

> Four tones of voice are generated by the varying specificity. The tone will be heard – if not consciously – by whoever reads. And the different tones give different information about the personality of the speaker as well as his state of mind. That is to say, the *I* generated in each sentence is different. (Delany 1969: 55)

Four differently constructed object noun phrases suggest four different personalities.

Character may be found to be alive and well in alternative world fiction if we look for it at the level of style as well as content. Interestingly, the link between character and style has come up from time to time in the critical literature on alternative world texts. In some cases, it seems to emerge almost by accident. A number of commentators, for example, begin by affirming the poor characterization thesis. Elsewhere in their argument, however, examples of convincing characterization arise spontaneously. What seems to be driving these spontaneous accounts is a reaction to language. Scholes (1975: 48), for example, accepted the view that 'psychological individuality' was often glossed over in alternative world texts to make way for the ideas expressed. Nevertheless, he found himself impressed with characterization in Le Guin's *The Left Hand of Darkness*. In his discussion of this text, it is clear that what he is reacting to is language. Le Guin's characters in this novel 'grow richer and more interesting to the very last words of the book' (89) for Scholes (1975), and one of the reasons why may be that 'we hear' (91) so many of their voices: 'the bardic voices of folk tellers, the cryptic voices of religious mysticism, and above all . . . the voices of the two main characters, who draw our human concern more intensely as the story progresses' (Scholes 1975: 91).

Roberts (2006) also seems to have found unlooked for characterization. In his opening chapter, he concedes to the prevailing view
that science fiction does not frequently offer detailed character studies
(112). In his chapter on technology, however, he offers numerous
examples of just such detailed studies, making a very convincing case
that robots and androids and other intelligent machines in a number
of texts are for all intents and purposes fully rounded characters.
As Meyers (1980: 9), Chatman (1978: 139), and Parrinder (1979b)
have noted, characters do not necessarily have to be human, or even
biological, to have convincing personalities, and what Roberts (2006:
112) observed with respect space ships applies equally well to the computers and artificial intelligences he also discusses. They 'are more
than machines, [they] can think for themselves, *express personality and
character*' (Roberts 2006: 112, italics mine). They not only have convincing personalities, but convincing personality disorders (Roberts
2006: 119). HAL, the computer in *2001: A Space Odyssey*, goes insane
(115). Marvin, the robot in *The Hitchhiker's Guide to the Galaxy*, is clini-
cally depressed (119). Behind these analyses seems to be a response
to the language of these constructs. For instance, when Roberts
(2006: 131) cites dialogue from Wintermute, a significant artificial
intelligence in *Neuromancer*, the quotes exhibit ordinary, informal
conversational English complete with slang. The artificial intelligence
may be compelling and believable as a character because it talks like
a person. His reaction to HAL (the computer in *2001: A Space Odyssey*)
seems similarly driven by language. The computer takes on human
traits largely through the way it talks, in 'a softly spoken, breathy and
warm voice that gains its sinister power in large part through how
"organic" it sounds' (Roberts 2006: 115).

In other cases, the link between character and style is more explicitly made, but the discussions stall when it comes to dealing with
the finer points of linguistic analysis. Timmerman (1983: 52) for
example, makes a connection between language and character in
The Lord of the Rings, saying that Tolkien's 'language is precise
and deliberate to the circumstance at hand in the story' (52). This
description, however, is not actually illuminating. The language of
a shopping list is also 'precise and deliberate to the circumstance at
hand.' Timmerman (1983) later qualifies his observation, narrowing

'precise and deliberate' down to 'appropriate diction' (52). This is an important insight – characters are often convincing because their language convinces. But *what* in the diction is appropriate? And what does 'appropriate' actually mean? Without sustained answers to these questions the initial insight is taken no further forward. Timmerman (1983: 52) finally demonstrates what he seems to mean in an example with Gollum, whose

> language is a hissing exhalation; an excess of slimy sibilants oozes out of his throat. Gollum is frightening yet Tolkien manages to evoke a deep pathos for this poor creature, stranded without love and friendship in the bowels of the mountain. (Timmerman 1983: 52)

While this goes some way towards fleshing out 'appropriate diction', no examples of these sibilants are given. In addition, no evidence is given for the second half of the observation, how 'Tolkien manages to evoke a deep pathos for Gollum'. What is it in the language that accomplishes this? Timmerman (1983) does not say.

Parrinder (1979b), intrigued by the idea of representing aliens with personalities, advances a link between this and style, but only tentatively. He mentions, without much elaboration, the issue of giving aliens different languages that are nevertheless understandable, and remarks several times that possession of language can be used to imply intelligence when representing aliens (e.g. see 151, 155 and 158). Again, however, we have here an example of a promising insight that is taken no further. Parrinder (1979b) leaves the issue of language at rest until the last page and a half of his article, where he briefly notes that aliens in science fiction can be given at least some sense of believable character 'by subjecting the writer's own language to a controlled stylistic distortion' (159). Indeed they can. Parrinder (1979b) is on to something here. Unfortunately, he leaves this observation undeveloped, as well. *What* stylistic distortions? In which aliens? And what do the distortions lead us to believe? Parrinder's (1979) account raises more questions than it answers.

If, like Toolan (1988) and Culpeper (2001) and others (e.g. Bennison 1993; Herman 1998; Myers 1983), we put a considered linguistic focus on the words used to construct character, we find that more revealing interpretations tend to emerge. One of the first things we discover is that alternative world texts may be more concerned with the inner lives of their characters than is typically noticed. This is evident in Robin Hobb's *Assassin's Apprentice*. As noted in Chapter 4 (where this work is also discussed), the story begins with the protagonist, Fitz, trying to write a history of his homeland. The task is a struggle, however, because painful memories from his childhood keep intruding. Born out of wedlock to a royal father and a mother of low birth, he is at first raised by his mother and her family. However, he is not really welcomed there, at least not by the real power of the family, his maternal grandfather. His grandfather eventually tires of caring for him and dumps him, at the age of six, on the doorstep of his father's stronghold, his mother's feeble protests echoing in the background.

> The old man lifted the brass knocker and banged it down, once, twice, thrice on the plate that resounded to his pounding. And then, from off-stage, a voice sounded. Not from within the doors, but from behind us, back the way we had come. 'Father, please,' the woman's voice begged. I turned to look at her, but it had begun to snow again, a lacy veil that clung to eyelashes and coatsleeves. I can't recall that I saw anyone. Certainly, I did not struggle to break free of the old man's grip on my hand, nor did I call out 'Mother, Mother!' Instead I stood, a spectator, and heard the sound of boots within the keep, and the unfastening of the door hasp within. (Hobb 1995: 3–4).

These narrated facts, and Fitz's own comments on them – 'the hurt of a boy' spilling out with the ink (2), 'shades of loneliness and loss' (2) – indicate the pain of isolation. However, *Assassin's Apprentice* does not stop with such self-presentations (instances of characters talking explicitly about themselves) (Culpeper 2001: 164). These can be unreliable, and thus unconvincing (Culpeper 2001: 164). It is through implicit textual clues, devices that prompt us to make inferences about personality, that character is most effectively revealed (Culpeper 2001: 164). *Assassin's Apprentice* is rich in such clues, and many of them are realized in plain, ordinary language. In the passage above and throughout chapter one, Fitz does not refer to members of his family with kinship terms (e.g., my mother, my granddad), but as strangers: 'the tall man' (3), 'the rangy old man who towered over me' (3), 'the old man' (3), 'the woman' (3). His only use of 'Mother' is in an account of what he did not say. Fitz describes his immediate family as though they were people he did not know. They are the same to him as the actual strangers he meets that day, 'the strange man with the bandaged leg' (12), and 'a stocky man' (6). Fitz's earliest memory is being delivered by strangers to strangers.

Noun phrases used to, about, or even by Fitz himself membership him as a burden or a problem. He is, variously, 'bastard' (15), 'a messy interruption' (6), 'boy' (8), 'this by-blow of yours' (14), 'his [father's] only failure' (19). By two different people in two different situations, he is received as a surprising object with the question '*What's* this?' (6 and 9, italics mine). Also telling is that the people Fitz knows are not, when he first mentions them, cast as active, doing agents.[3] He does not recall his mother as actively crying out on his behalf; rather, he remembers her as an unknown, unfamiliar voice: 'A voice sounded' (3). Neither, from Fitz's perspective, does his grandfather hold his hand. He describes this action mostly as just a hand that holds his: 'the huge hand that gripped my small one' (3); 'my small hand trapped inside the tall man's' (3). Such to Fitz is his family – a distant voice, a mysterious hand.

Casting body parts as agents in this way has the effect of distancing Fitz from his own family and suggests that he has trouble interpreting how others feel about him. A number of Fitz's informing speech acts reinforce this trait. Reports of actions tend to be clear, and his certainty about them reinforced with intensifiers (italicized in the examples):

Certainly, I did not struggle to break free of the old man's grip on my hand, nor did I call out, 'Mother, Mother!';(4)

I remember *quite clearly* how he went down on one knee to tug my shirt straight and smooth my hair with a rough pat or two. (6)

Reports of emotions, however, are recalled as unsolved mysteries:

> whether this was from some kind-hearted impulse that I make
> a good impression, or merely a concern that his package look
> well-tended, I shall never know; (6)
> A tremor shook the hand that gripped mine, but whether of anger
> or some other emotion, I shall never know. (4)

The language of Fitz's memories – ordinary, usual, non-deviant, not
particularly noticeable, nevertheless allows readers to infer something about his character that he himself has not figured out: his
urge to explain himself (2). Children who are wanted and loved are
not strangers in their own lives. Their presence is welcomed and
accepted. They enter the world and immediately belong, and the
need to explain themselves is not even thought of, let alone required.
Fitz, clearly, is in a different situation. In the alternative world of
Assassin's Apprentice, Fitz is a 'royal bastard'. Psychologically, however,
he is recognizable in modern terms as an unwanted stepchild.

Something of the inner life of Gunpat Smith, the protagonist of 'A
Spot of Konfrontation', is also revealed through careful but non-
obvious manipulations of style. Classified as a somewhat reluctant
speaker of spEEC in Chapter 2 (see pages 58–67), Gunpat is described
in 'Konfrontation' as 'a slender brown man with nervous gestures'
(78). And so he is. He hurries (78), peers anxiously behind him
(78), and smiles too hard (79). There is, however, a bit more to
him, and this is conveyed through the device of free indirect discourse. In free indirect discourse, third person reports of speech
or thought are delivered as though they were first person reports
(Baldick 1990: 87). As Toolan (1988: 116) puts it, free indirect
discourse takes 'external facts about a character' and seamlessly
combines them with their 'intimate thoughts', as in this example
from 'Konfrontation':

> Smith lay absolutely still, trying to decide whether he could bear to
> get up off the bed; he saw by his watch that he had been asleep
> for under two hours.

> The effort had to be made. How few actions in this world were
> voluntary! (80)

A number of Gunpat's thoughts are revealed in this way:

> Her unreliability was such a blemish – and so inevitable in the
> circumstances! (79)
> His life alternatives were social degradation in the UK after next
> week, or exile in Tahiti forever! (87)
> None of the ghastly things that had happened since could take that
> experience away from him! (92)
> How dismally significant the name had proved! (92)
> Life wasn't always so full incident. You could say that. (92)

These represented thoughts share a number of features. They
are, for example, all relatively formal. They are all grammatically
complete and they all exhibit a concentration of learned, Latinate
vocabulary suggestive of precision (*voluntary, inevitable, incident, significant, alternatives*). Many of them are delivered as exclamations.
Gradually and indirectly, it is revealed that Gunpat is not only
nervous, but fussy, pedantic, and excitable.

It has thus far been demonstrated that linguistic analysis can reveal
complex characterization at work in alternative world texts. With
language at the heart of the analysis, it is also easier to see that flat
characters can be just as valuable as round ones. As Chatman (1978:
132) has noted, there is no necessary connection between a flat
character and a poorly drawn one, or flat characterization and weak
characterization. Flat characters can be just as interesting as round
ones, a point that Forster (1927) seems to have been aware of, as well.
While he notes that flat characters may not be much of an achievement (77), he acknowledges that novels need both types of character
(76), and seems most interested in the flat ones. He spends more time
discussing them, and defines them carefully. Round characters, on
the other hand, are, by his own admission, defined mostly 'by implication' (80) as not flat. He also gives examples of flat characters that
contribute as much to a work as round ones, although this seems to

perplex him. Discussing Dickens, Forster (1927/2000: 76) claims that
'he ought to be bad' because he uses so many flat characters. And yet
he is not. He is one of the greats (Forster 1927/2000: 76):

> He uses types and caricatures, people whom we recognise the
> instant they re-enter, and yet he achieves effects that are not
> mechanical and a vision of humanity that is not shallow. (Forster
> 1927/2000: 76)

As Chatman (1978) observed and Forster (1927) himself realized,
flat characters can be just as effective and well-drawn as round ones.

Alternative world fiction may indeed be full of flat characters, as
the critical literature on these texts insists *ad nauseam*. A linguistic
analysis, however, demonstrates that these flat characters can still be
compelling, both in terms of depiction and effect. This is apparent in
Aldiss's 'Amen and Out'. As noted previously in Chapter 4 where this
story was also discussed, 'Amen and Out' relates an incident at the
Immortality Investigation Project, an organization that claims to
house and care for, but in reality imprisons and exploits, a group of
citizens who are able to live indefinitely long. The Project is interesting, it can be argued, not only because of what goes on there, but also
because of some of the characters connected with it, Jaybert Darkling,
a manager; Zee Stone, a junior member of his staff; and Dean Cusak,
a doorman. All of these characters are flat. They can be 'expressed in
one sentence' (Forster 1927/2000: 73). Darkling is a hypocrite (53),
Zee Stone blames other for faults in himself (54), and Dean Cusak is
a hen-pecked 'yes-man' (55). This flatness, however, is not a narrative
weakness that needs excusing. While each of these characters may
have only one trait, the language given to them presents a complex
dissection of that trait, allowing the story to explore the nature of
hypocrisy, self-delusion and internalized oppression. Notice, for
example, (in Table 5.1 below) how Darkling, Cusak and Stone 'pray'
to their 'gods' (actually personal computers as noted in Chapter 4).

Of all these first prayers, Darkling's is the most formal and the one
closest to ritual religious language. The opening address, Almighty
Gods, is (apart from the plural), typical of prayer, and the closing
Amen is standard. Darkling also expresses that which he prays for in

Table 5.1 First prayers of Darkling, Stone and Cusak in 'Amen and Out'

Darkling	Cusak	Stone
'Almighty Gods, I come before you at the start of another day dedicated to your purposes. Grant that I may in every way fulfil myself by acting according to your law and walking in your ways. Amen.' (53)	'Almighty Gods, help me. I'm a terrible worm, she's right, a terrible worm. You know me, you know what I am. Help me – it's not that I haven't struggled, you know I've struggled, but things are going from bad to worse. I've always served you, tried to do your will, Gods, don't let me down!' (55–56)	'I suppose I'm due for my usual bawling out!' (54)
'I will do differently today, Almighty Gods. I will spend the day working at the project, which is surely dedicated to your ends' (53)	'Yes, Gods, thanks, I will, I will, I'll do exactly as you say – but . . . how?' (56)	'You know everything – you know why it was. I'm trying to write a story. I want to be a writer. But everytime I begin, even if I have it all planned out, it turns into a different story. You're doing it, aren't you?' (54)
'Your will be done' (53)		'To hell with that!' (54)

the typical language of recited prayer (*Grant that I may . . .*), and employs a concentration of terms that suggests religious duty: *purposes, fulfil, according to, law* and *will* (both as a verb of promising, and a noun). Also included are a cluster of formulae familiar from or based on Christian religious texts: *I come before you, acting according to your law, walking in your ways, your will be done.* Built from familiar religious language, Darkling's prayer is the most prayer-like, but also the one that comes across as the most rehearsed; consequently, it is the prayer that sounds the least sincere. Hypocrite that he is, he parades all the right words, but there is no real intention behind them. It just sounds good.

Darkling's response to the gods, *I will do differently today* (53), is similarly empty. As the speech act of promising, it is infelicitous since one of it constituting conditions (Searle 1969) is violated. As Searle (1969: 57–61) explains, one of the things that makes a promise a promise is that speakers cannot promise to do something they would do 'in the normal course of events' anyway. One cannot, for example, promise to breathe. As Myers (1983: 306), through Searle (1979), notes, a speech act made in fiction has no status in the real world, but is nevertheless treated in the same way. An insincere promise in fiction is likely to tell us something about the fictional promiser in the same way an insincere promise in the real world would, and this is what happens with Darkling's promise. By 'doing differently', he means 'working at the project.' While the Project may (or may not) fulfil the purpose of the gods, his promise to go there and work is entirely void, since he would do that anyway in the normal course of events as a paid employee. Darkling sounds like he is making a promise but again, it only sounds good. There is no substance behind it.

Darkling also has several long speeches in the story, and these might at first be dismissed as the 'expository lumps' so reviled in pulp-style. In the following extract from one of his longer turns at talk, for example, he expounds at length on the nature of the Immortals.

> The Immortals have been cut off from man's root drives. For obvious reasons, the only drives we can inherent are those that manifest themselves before reproduction. It was argued in times past, quite dogmatically, that there were no other drives. Well, we see differently now. We see that once through the senility barrier, man is no longer a doing creature but a thinking creature [. . .]. (60)

While this does provide useful background information to the events and issues in the story, its primary purpose, arguably, is characterization rather than exposition. When the language of this speech is considered, we discover that it tells us more about Darkling and his hypocrisy than the Immortals. Although this is a reply in a conversation, it sounds more like a quote from a formal address or a textbook than spontaneous talk. Many of the sentences are complex, with multiple clauses (*we can inherit; that manifest themselves before reproduction; that there were no other drives; that . . . man is a no longer a doing creature, but a thinking creature*) that allow for a denser information load that is more typical of writing than speech (Brown and Yule 1987). All of the sentences are grammatically complete, and the scientific passive voice (Crystal 1988: 75) is used (*it was argued*). There are none of the normal elisions and hesitation devices that characterize normal conversation and other markers of ordinary talk, such as common conversational routines and vague language, are similarly absent. Interestingly, 'synthetic personalisation' devices used to imply an immediately present and intimate audience when none exists, such as the use of *we* and the discourse marker *well* (Fairclough 1995: 80), are used. These ring especially false, as Darkling actually does have an immediately present and intimate audience there – his interlocutor Zee Stone. As he was in his prayer, Darkling is here simply too polished and too rehearsed. He parades the stock answer with no true commitment. Darkling's language simultaneously reveals both the falseness of his position, and his attempt to maintain it. The pious dedicated professional is an illusion, and it is the style, the way language is used in the story, that leads us not only to see the mask, but to see through it.

Darkling's language also shows us one of the unfortunate side effects of hypocrisy. Too weak and morally bankrupt, being a hypocrite, to lead by good example, Darkling often resorts to threats (*You watch your step, Stone! Don't think I don't know of your activities with Miss Roberts when you should be on duty*, 69); insults (*You fool, Stone!*, 69; *You crafty little bastard!*, 69); accusations (*You're trying to trick me, aren't you?*, 69), and shouted orders (*get out of my office!*, 69; *Get out!*, 69; *Get out at once and never come in here again!*, 69).

Dean Cusak's prayer shows us a man crippled by anxiety and an almost complete lack of confidence. His language encourages the inference that he actively seeks victim status. His requestives are all appeals for help (*help me; don't let me down*), and his informatives offer justifications (*You know me, you know what I am; it's not that I haven't struggled, you know that I've struggled; things have gone from bad to worse*); seek approval (*I've always served you, tried to do your will*); or express self-criticism (*I'm a terrible worm*). Of all the characters that pray, Cusak is the only one to suffer the indignity of being cut off by the gods in mid-prayer (56), and this he meekly accepts as his due.

Cusak's language also conveys a sense of helpless desperation. His prayer is a torrent of anxiety, an effect that is created by using a number of simple structures and joining them in simple ways. Many of the clauses used are short and independent, with only one subject and verb (*Almighty Gods, help me; Gods, don't let me down; you know me; I've always served you*), and sometimes less than that (*Help me;*

a terrible worm). Coordination, the joining of simple independent units like links in a chain (*Almighty Gods, help me. I'm a terrible worm, she's right, a terrible worm! You know me*) is more salient in the prayer than subordination, and embedded clauses when they do occur are simple and limited to one per sentence (*what I am; that I haven't struggled; that I've struggled; as you say*). Cusak runs to his gods in a panic, and his state of mind is conveyed to us through his language. His prayer tumbles out in a spontaneous rush.

The language of Cusak's prayer, appropriate to his one trait, also stands in stark contrast to Darkling's. Yes-man he may be, but Cusak is no hypocrite. While his prayer exhibits far less of the formal religious language that characterized Darkling's, it nevertheless comes across as more sincere. It draws largely on Old English and Germanic vocabulary, words familiar and known that, as Wright and Hope (1996: 215) point out, spring spontaneously to the lips, especially at times of high emotion (see also Adamson 1989). Other features suggesting the immediacy of private conversation are also present. Apart from *Almighty Gods* and *a terrible worm*, all of the noun phrases in the prayer are unmodified and mostly consist of simple pronouns (*I, me, she, you, it*). In addition, there are conversational routines (*Yes, thanks*), fixed phrases (*don't let me down; from bad to worse*), and vague language (*things*). Cusak's prayer, offered without pretence or guile, is an honest heart-to-heart with his gods. Next to Cusak's sincerity, Darkling's hypocrisy looks even worse.

Zee Stone's trait, a tendency to blame others for faults in himself, is displayed through what Brown and Levinson (1978/1987) have called *re-ranking*. According to Brown and Levinson (1978/1987: 74), speakers take into account three sociocultural variables when deciding on how, or even whether, to address someone. These variables they call power (P), distance (D) and rank of imposition (R). When the relationship between speaker and hearer is asymmetric, as Brown and Levinson (1978/1987: 74) observe, P is an important factor in the language they choose to use. Employees, for example, will speak differently to their bosses than to their friends, and employers will speak differently to their staff than to their peers. When the relationship is equal, D becomes more important. People speak one way to strangers, and another to those they know well. R refers to how much or how little your goal or reason for speaking will impose on your hearer. If you ask to borrow your friend's pen, for example, you are likely to phrase your request in one way. If you ask to borrow their car, you may well ask in another (Brown and Levinson 1978/ 1987: 74). As Brown and Levinson (1978/1987: 229) go on to note, speakers can exploit these variables by re-ranking them, behaving linguistically as though P, D, and R were greater or lesser than in actual fact they are.

This kind of re-ranking is demonstrated in Zee Stone's prayer, and shows us the lengths to which he will go to avoid dealing with his own faults. He comes before his gods having sinned, but is not contrite. His confession, if such it can be called, shows neither respect nor remorse. Instead, he re-ranks power and the gravity of his imposition, in this case his sins, and behaves as though the problem is the gods' tendency to interfere rather than his own poor behaviour (*I suppose I'm due for my usual bawling out!*). When the gods identify precisely Stone's fault ('All that happens within you, you try to blame on things outside. That way you will never prosper', 57), his response shows another re-ranking of power. As a supplicant addressing his gods, Stone's speech situation is just about as asymmetric as it gets. However, he behaves linguistically as though he and the gods were on an equal footing, dismissing their warning with an aggravated rejection (*To hell with that!*).

Darkling, Cusak and Stone are flat, one dimensional characters, governed by one trait alone. They represent human universals and in doing so prompt us to ask questions about human nature. Such an interpretation, however, does not have to be offered as an excuse for, or in spite of, poor characterization. While the characters in 'Amen and Out' are flat, they are still compelling. Darkling can be summed up as a hypocrite, but he is an utterly consistent and convincing hypocrite. Dean Cusak may be no more than a yes-man, but he is that yes-man through and through. Stone is so self-deluding one wants to shake some sense into him (I did, at any rate). An account of alternative world fiction based on the assumption that character, as a rule, is poorly handled in these texts, will certainly find flat characters in 'Amen and Out', but will miss the point. As the linguistic analysis offered here has shown, flat characters are not by definition poorly drawn.

Aldiss provides another example of flat characterization in 'Three Ways' (discussed briefly in Chapter 4, page 107). In this story, a group of space travellers return to Earth but find it much changed from when they left. In their absence, there has been a series of violent climatic and political catastrophes, including an ice age and two nuclear wars, resulting in the reduction of all the world's nations to only five areas, Corporatia, Socdemaria, Communia, Neutralia and Third World. As their ship orbits Earth, the travellers are briefed on the changes that have occurred by a representative of Corporatia. This representative is so clearly flat that she could serve as a textbook example. Described only as 'a plain-faced woman' (28), she is never named. She can be reduced to a single sentence, 'She represents Corporatia.' She is not only metaphorically flat but, in the world of the story, actually flat. The travellers see only her image on screen. This flattest of flat characters, however, invites immediate and thorough distrust, an effect created through subtle contrasts in style.

As the travellers are briefed, they are shown documentary footage of what transpired while they were away. The description of these images in the narration is detailed and vivid. The horror of what occurred is recounted, as we would expect in this situation, in the active voice, which makes the subject apparent and puts it where it is expected at the front of the clause: 'gigantic slabs of ice launched themselves off the Irish coast' (29); 'walls of metal glowed and came thunderously together' (29); 'nuclear explosions billowed outwards ' (30); 'metal men marched, storming down tunnels to subterranean cities' (30). Working with the active voice in some of these passages are strings of non-finite verbs, verbs that occur without tense (e.g. *running* or *to run*). In the passage below, where they are italicized, they emphasize the chaotic nature of the events, creating for the reader the same experience created for the characters, encountering one shocking event after another without time to integrate them into an organized sequence of events:

Rioting, violent clashes between civilians and fleet armoured vehicles, fire-cannon *shooting* down vast underground streets, tanks *shovelling* aside bodies, rocketships *plunging* like daggers into the lunar crust, heads *flying* from bodies under the sweep of a machine

with horizontal blades, lines of missiles *darkening* a china blue sky.
(30, italics mine)

The report of these events delivered by the spokeswoman of
Corporatia is syntactically different. Her account makes heavy use
of the passive voice (italicized in the examples given), which de-
emphasizes or conceals entirely the subject, the acting agent in
the clause: 'Climatic disturbances *have* inevitably *been followed* by
civil disturbances. These *have been quelled*, often with considerable
loss of life'; 'you *will be issued* with regulations'; 'restrictions *will be
lifted* as soon as the emergency is over' (29–30); 'you may find your
own country . . . *has been entirely reorganised*' (30) 'you *will be dispersed*
according to your appropriate democratic area' (29). Who quelled
the disturbances, exactly? And who reorganized the countries? Who
will issue the regulations and disperse the returning cosmonauts?
The woman neatly avoids these issues. The syntactic manipulation
from active to passive show us a spokesperson who appears to be
dodging the issue of ultimate responsibility.

In conjunction with her use of the passive voice, the woman
also asserts things that are, apparently, necessary, as in 'it has been
necessary to reintroduce capital punishment' (30), and 'severe
curtailments of individual liberty have been necessary in the public
interest' (30). While these are not syntactically the passive voice,
they do a similar job in hiding agency (Greenbaum and Quirk
1990: 360) by keeping the focus on what became necessary, instead
of who decided that it was necessary.

The woman's use of the passive voice and related structures allows
her to gloss over the catastrophic events with a degree of distance and
false calm. By hiding agency and keeping the focus on the events,
the woman can speak as though she were just listing a series of dry,
dull facts. Given the horror of what actually happened, the woman's
attempts to conceal are gross. In Forster's (1927/2000: 74) terms,
this is what makes her memorable to the 'reader's emotional eye', a
particular feature of flat characters. She stands for deception, and
this deception is communicated through style.

Aldiss is acknowledged as an accomplished stylist in a number
of places (e.g. see Mathews 1977; Stockwell 2000), and he is also

considered an able creator of character. McNelly (1982: 252), for example, speaks admiringly of his 'depth of characterisation', Mathews (1977: 5) praises his 'creation of believable and rounded human characters', and Henighan (1999: 115) describes Aldiss's later work as 'character-based in a powerful way.' Few of Aldiss's comment-ators, however, have put style and character creation together, and fewer still have taken any interest in what are, as this analysis has shown, his skilfully drawn and convincing flat characters.

Three of the *Star Trek* spin-offs, *Enterprise, The Next Generation (TNG)* and *Voyager*, offer a particularly fascinating case of flat characteriza-tion in The Borg, the great enemy of the United Federation of Planets. The Borg are part humanoid, part cybernetic beings who exist as a collective, analogous to a colony of ants or a hive of bees. While there are billions of individuals in the Collective, they share a single consciousness. Existing only as drones, single Borg have no sense of themselves as individuals and are controlled entirely by the will of the Collective. There is no self-determination, no freedom, no concept of living an independent life. The Borg have no names, only designations. There is no emotion, only logic and efficiency. If one drone dies, there is no grief, no ceremony, no sense of loss. What remains of them is reabsorbed into the Collective, and another drone simply takes its place.

The Borg Collective is a flat character. It is motivated by one thing and one thing only, the ruthless and forcible assimilation of entire cul-tures and their technologies. The Collective does nothing else. It is this very flatness, however, that makes the Borg interesting. Their literal single-mindedness is what makes them such a formidable enemy. As Jean Luc Picard, Captain of the starship Enterprise in *TNG*, puts it,

> In their collective state, the Borg are utterly without mercy, driven by one will alone, the will to conquer. They are beyond redemption, beyond reason. (Captain Janeway quoting from Picard's personal log in the *Voyager* episode 'Scorpion, Part 1')[4]

The language given to the Borg is a convincing extrapolation of how such a ruthless and inhumane Collective might communicate. Apart from a few exceptions,[5] individual Borg are not shown speaking. Their collective voice, many voices speaking as one, is simply heard. As the following representative examples of Borg speech illustrate, they have a relentlessly factual and command-driven way of speaking:

> You will be assimilated. Resistance if futile; (*Enterprise*, 'Regeneration')
>
> We have analyzed your defensive capabilities as being unable to withstand us. If you defend yourselves, you will be punished; (*TNG*, 'Q Who?')
>
> Freedom is irrelevant. Self-determination is irrelevant. You must comply; (*TNG*, 'The Best of Both Worlds, Part 1')
>
> Strength is irrelevant. Resistance if futile. We wish to improve ourselves. We will add your biological and technological distinctiveness to our own. Your culture will adapt to service ours; (*TNG*, 'The Best of Both Worlds, Part 1')
>
> Jean Luc Picard Captain of the Starship Enterprise Registry NCC 1701D. You will lower your shields and prepare to transport yourself aboard our vessel. If you do not cooperate we will destroy your ship; (*TNG*, 'The Best of Both Worlds, Part 1')
>
> We are the Borg. Existence as you know it is over. We will add your biological and technological distinctiveness to our own. (*Voyager*, 'Scorpion, Part 1')

Most of the Borg speech acts are of two types, informatives such as facts, assessments and statements of intentions (*Self-determination is irrelevant*; *We have analysed your defensive capabilities as being unable to withstand us*), or directives, mostly commands and threats (*You will lower your shields and prepare to transport yourself aboard our vessel*; *If you defend yourselves, you will be punished*). (My speech act definitions, here and throughout, are based on Tsui 1994.) They are concerned only to express their will and their speech correspondingly makes little use of features that accommodate their interlocutors. For example, they make little use of greetings and leave-takings. When they do address an interlocutor directly at the start of an interaction, they do not express goodwill but simply identify with precision (*Jean Luc Picard, Captain of the Starship Enterprise Registry NCC 1701D*). They make few true responses (see note 6 for this chapter), reacting to others mostly by repeating their own initial statements and commands. They do nothing to build solidarity or rapport with their interlocutors. As a result, positive politeness devices, the linguistic elements that realize such cooperative impulses (Brown and Levinson 1978/1987), are absent from their speech. They do not, for example, make jokes, offer compliments, express gratitude, or enquire about the welfare of others. Neither do they do anything that indicates respect for or courtesy towards their interlocutors. This leads to a corresponding absence of negative politeness devices, such as indicating reluctance to impose on others (Brown and Levinson 1978/1987). The Borg do not, for instance, hedge their assessments, or attempt to minimize their intrusions. They do not, for example, say 'Death is *kind of* irrelevant' or '*We know this is difficult for you, but* we will add your biological and technological distinctiveness to our own. *Don't worry, it only hurts a little.*' Their speech acts are what Brown and Levinson (1978/1987: 60) term 'bald-on-record' delivered with 'maximum efficiency' and no regard for the interlocutor.

Nothing indicating human community or emotion enters Borg speech. They do not hesitate or make false starts or use filled pauses (*um, er*, etc.). Their speech shows no variation. They have no slang, no dialects, no linguistic traces of class or gender. They do not gossip or make small talk. They do not have differing public and private speech styles. They do not play with language. They have no irony, no sarcasm, no idioms, no understatement or overstatement. Their speech is devoid of the spontaneous literary devices typical of talk (Tannen 1989), such as metaphors and similes. They do not intensify or aggravate their speech acts (e.g. 'You *really, really* MUST comply'), and they have no need to demonize their enemies. They do not say, for example, *We will shoot you out of the sky, you scum!* They simply announce their will. Borg speech, both in terms of what it does and does not do, represents a plausible vision of how a single consciousness dedicated solely to forcible assimilation might talk. That the Borg Collective is flat in terms of characterization does not detract from the stylistic achievement that is their speech.

Borg speech is interesting for another reason, as well. When it is compared to some of the human dialogue, similarities become apparent instead of the expected differences. In the extract below, for example, it can be argued that the dialogue of the Enterprise crew is closer to Borg speech than human interaction in a number of ways. Commander Riker, temporarily promoted to Captain, is instructing the crew on the ship's bridge, the command centre of the Enterprise.

Riker:	Reset subspace communications, scrambler code Riker One.
Crew Member:	Scrambler code Riker One acknowledged.
Riker:	Shelby, report.
Shelby:	Ready for separation.
Riker:	Make it so.
Shelby:	Auto subsequence initiated.
La Forge:	Docking latches clear. Separation complete.
Ensign Crusher:	Saucer velocity 100 meters per second and increasing, Sir.
Riker:	Open fire. All weapons.
Shelby:	Fire. (*TNG*, 'The Best of Both Worlds, Part 2')

The language here, like the Borg speech analysed earlier, consists mostly of commands (*Make it so*; *Reset subspace communications*) and informatives (*Separation complete*; *Docking latches clear*). With the exception of 'sir', the utterances are bald-on-record, with neither positive nor negative politeness devices. The focus is entirely on the task at hand and attitudinal or affective elements (understatement, overstatement, slang, variation, etc.) are absent. It would be inaccurate to assert that all the bridge interactions in *TNG* are like this. They are not, as the human characters in the program speak like humans. However, the Borg-like militaristic precision in bridge interactions is not rare, either. This noticeable convergence may serve as a quiet reminder that the United Federation of Planets differs from its enemy the Borg only in degree, as several commentators have noted (e.g. see Consalvo 2004: 196; Jackson and Nexon 2003: 164; Kavanagh et al. 2001; Short 2004). The Federation, an analogue for the United States and Western military and political alliances (e.g., NATO, the UN), is, after all, an assimilating force. It works by treaty, negotiation, and its much-disobeyed Prime Directive (the principle of not interfering with the development of other cultures), but it is arguably just as relentless as the Borg, flying through space attempting to unite other worlds under its own sphere of influence.

A linguistic study of the dialogue in *Star Trek* also reveals a feature of characterization of interest to alternative world fiction but not particularly salient in realist fiction. This is the narrative situation of flat characters that journey towards becoming round. The *Star Trek TNG* episode 'I, Borg' explores this issue in some detail. In this episode, the crew of the Enterprise find a single Borg that is alone and severely wounded. The ship's doctor insists on treating him, and he is brought aboard. At first, he behaves in typical Borg fashion. After he is sufficiently recovered, he announces, 'We are Borg. You will be assimilated. Resistance is futile.' As time goes on, however, he begins to develop both a sense of individuality and humanity, and the crew eventually give him a name, Hugh. Unlike the Borg in the Collective, Hugh ceases to be dominated by the will to assimilate. This is evident in his use of questions, which show curiosity and evidence of learning.

'What is Geordi doing?'
'What is a doctor?'
'Why?'
'Do I have a name?'

Unlike the collective Borg, Hugh wants to know about the world, not assimilate it.

With his link to the Collective severed, Hugh's speech becomes more truly interactive. He greets others ('Hello, Geordi'), and contributes to conversational exchanges by responding to others appropriately. In the exchange below, for example, he positively responds.[6]

Geordi: Hugh, I'd like to take a closer look at your eye piece. Is that okay?
Hugh: [Obliges] Here.
Geordi: Thanks.

In another interaction with Geordie, he responds positively to Geordie's assessment (of what a friend is) by making a similar assessment (that he and Geordie are friends):

Geordie: Sure. Someone you can talk to. Who'll be with you when you are lonely. Someone . . . someone who makes you feel better.
Hugh: Like Geordi and Hugh.

He also continues to expand his repertoire of speech act types. In addition to asking questions, he makes requests for confirmation. That is, he states what he supposes to be the case and invites his interlocutor to confirm it.

> Hugh: When you sleep, there are no other voices in your mind.
> Geordi: No.

Hugh's language also begins to show a concern for others, and a growing understanding that the Borg way is not the only way. This is evident in his informatives, which display his attempt to explain his point of view without menace by relating it to the experience of his human interlocutors.

> Hugh: Here it is quiet. There are no other voices.
> Geordi: Other voices?
> Hugh: On a Borg ship we live with the thoughts of the others on our minds. Thousands of voices with us always.

Hugh also uses the positive politeness device of presupposing knowledge of his hearer's wants and attitudes (Brown and Levinson 1978/1987: 122), and successfully makes a connection with an initially hostile interlocutor, a woman named Guinan whose people were nearly annihilated by the Borg.

> Guinan: My people resisted when the Borg came to assimilate us. Some of us survived.
> Hugh: Resistance is not futile?
> Guinan: No. But thanks to you, there are very few of us left. We're scattered throughout the galaxy. We don't even have a home anymore.
> Hugh: What you are saying is that you are lonely.
> Guinan: [incredulous] What?
> Hugh: You have no others. You have no home. We are also lonely.

In his final two utterances above, Hugh asserts knowledge of Guinan's needs and feelings (*What you are saying is that you are lonely; You have no others; You have no home*), and stresses their common experience (*We are also lonely*).

Hugh's journey towards individuality is also charted in his use of personal pronouns. When first aboard the Enterprise, he speaks of himself as Borg in the first person plural ('We are Borg'). Gradually, however, this changes. When he is given a name, he speaks of himself with that name, although he retains the first person plural ('We are Hugh'). By the end of the episode, however, he has, as the Star Trek crew do not fail to notice, become 'a fully realised individual', and he asserts that individuality with the first person singular ('I am Hugh').

In this chapter, the linguistic analyses performed have allowed for a re-evaluation of character and characterization in alternative world fiction. It has been shown that alternative world texts can and do convincingly present round characters. In addition, it has been demonstrated that flat characters are not necessarily thinly drawn ones. A representative type can be just as compelling in alternative world fiction as a represented person. The focus on language has also revealed what may be a particularity of alternative world texts, the exploration of flat characters in the process of becoming round. Contrary to what the prevailing view of these texts would have us believe, character thrives in alternative world fiction when we look for it as an illusion of style rather than content.

Chapter 6

Style in Alternative World Texts: Conclusion

Alternative world texts have had something of a long, hard climb on the road to academic respectability. In the main, the journey has been a successful one and a number of myths once widely associated with them have long since been put to rest. Gone are the days when these texts were dismissed out of hand as juvenile and escapist brain candy. In this book, I have shown that one last myth, however, has remained: the myth that alternative world texts fall short, often miserably so, when it comes to style. This myth has been remarkably persistent, overriding arguments and evidence that have, from time to time, emerged in opposition. In the preceding chapters, it has been my purpose to lay this last remaining myth to rest by presenting a series of literary-linguistic analyses showing that style in alternative world fiction is not poor or merely adequate, but essential, integral, and effective. Chapter 2 looked at three very different alternative world texts that all used experimental prose to make English itself strange in order to challenge English-only or English-dominant complacencies and assumptions. Texts that rupture the language of their telling have also to ensure that this language is still comprehensible, and the role of style in successfully maintaining this balance was also investigated in this chapter. While Chapter 2 tackled the claim that alternative world texts tend to avoid experiments in linguistic form, Chapters 4 and 5 challenged the frequently touted assumption that plain language in alternative world fiction is proof of a weak or pedestrian style. In a number of analyses covering a range of texts, Chapter 4 demonstrated that very ordinary linguistic features, such as simple noun phrases and prepositional phrases, are nevertheless vital elements of style serving to present the unreal and the incredible as the actual and the already believed. That effects with plain language are easy to miss does not make them dismissible.

Continuing the exploration of plain language, Chapter 5 illustrated that character, long thought to be a particularly weak aspect of alternative world fiction, is in many cases a strength. Careful attention to style showed that round characters, contrary to popular belief, do appear in the pages of alternative world texts, and that flat characters, while also evident, are no less compelling. Style in alternative world fiction, it was further shown, also served to create a particularly interesting character type, the flat character that becomes round over time.

Sitting between the first two chapters and the last two chapters thematically as well as numerically, Chapter 3 looked at the use of archaic language in alternative world texts. Archaic forms, it was shown, were a very effective means of bringing a coherent and convincing past world to life in the narrative. This was true not only of grammatical and lexical items, but also of pragmatic units such as speech acts and forms of address. Often evaluated negatively as clumsy affectations, this study showed instead that old style greetings, leave-takings, expressions of gratitude and other formulaic acts in alternative world texts were often genuine archaisms that not only opened a door to the created past world, but suggested a community of speakers at home in that world. As also demonstrated in Chapter 3, archaic forms are deviant forms in present-day English, and their use entails the same attention to comprehensibility as the experimental Englishes discussed in Chapter 2.

As the studies in this book have shown, alternative world texts do not necessarily avoid experiments in form, and when they do use 'plain' language, that language is still stylistically effective. Style extrapolates future Englishes, suggests spoken past Englishes, presents the impossible as real and creates characters. No longer should it be dismissed or explained away as an embarrassment. It is my hope that future studies of alternative world fiction will build on this one in further elucidating the essential aspect that is style.

Notes

Chapter 1

1 Meyers (1980: 34) is speaking here about the use of archaic pronouns in Quaker speech communities.

Chapter 2

1 While Short (1989) speaks in terms of communication between the playwright and the audience, I am more comfortable with the notion of the audience, or reader, being in contact with the text.

2 An earlier version of the *Firefly* analysis appeared in 'Chinese and Code-Switching in Firefly', chapter three of *Investigating* Firefly *and* Serenity: *Science Fiction on the Frontier* (edited by Wilcox and Cochrane) London: I.B. Tauris.

3 As Westfahl's (2003) discussion indicates, many science fiction narratives deal with the theme of Asian influence or control in some proposed US or broader Western future. It is discussions of the way that language works to convey such futures that are, I suggest, relatively rare.

4 I am grouping together under the term 'net-slang' what appears to be a continuum of varieties spoken by the VR users. Explicit mention is made in *Otherland* of at least two sub-varieties that the characters themselves seem to differentiate, 'kidspeak', spoken by young children, and 'goggleboy', an extreme variety spoken by 'charge heads' who use the properties of VR as a drug.

5 The Chinese borrowings in *Otherland* are confirmed by Tad Williams himself in his posts on the official, publisher maintained *Tad Williams Website*, http://www.tadwilliams.com). While an attempt was made to cross-check these borrowings, this was only possible with *fen*, since the spellings used in the novel do not consistently employ pinyin.

6 Tad Williams identifies *seen* as a Rastafarian/Caribbean borrowing in one of his posts on the official, publisher maintained *Tad Williams Website* (http://www.tadwilliams.com).

7 This, as Tad Williams notes in one of his posts on the official, publisher maintained *Tad Williams Website* (http://www.tadwilliams.com), is a version of the British English word *cheers*.

[8] I am drawing here on insights from Braj Kachru, who has argued in several places that many varieties of English around the world, particularly second language varieties, are developing independently.

[9] My analysis here is informed by *Contact Languages*, Mark Sebba's (1997) thorough and comprehensive account of pidgin and creole languages.

[10] Work in sociolinguistics (e.g. see LePage and Tabouret-Keller 1985) has shown that pidgin languages can often be used as in-group languages, and analyses of pidgins represented in literature have been analysed in light of such findings (see Traugott 1981). However, there was no evidence in 'Konfrontation' that spEEC was used as an in-group language.

[11] I am indebted to my colleague Gilbert Ockton for pointing me in the right direction with *rummet, reviendra* and *als*.

[12] There are a few cases were it also seems to mean 'our'.

[13] SpEEC bears a superficial resemblance to various artificial languages, most notably Esperanto, so it might be argued that one of its purposes is to comment in some way on such languages. The pidginization argument advanced here, however, fits more closely with the organic nature of the language as evidenced in the text.

Chapter 3

[1] This edition includes *The Dreaming City*, 1961; *While the Gods Laugh*, 1962; *The Stealer of Souls*, 1962; *Kings in Darkness*, 1962; *The Caravan of Forgotten Dreams*, 1962; *Stormbringer*, 1965, 1977.

[2] This edition includes 'The People of the Black Circle', 1934; 'The Slithering Shadow', 1933; and 'The Pool of the Black One', 1933. A fourth Conan story, 'Drums of Tombalku' is included in the collection, but since it was begun by Howard and finished by L. Sprague de Camp, it has not been analysed here.

[3] I have drawn on a number of helpful sources throughout this chapter on the history of English, including Atherton (2006); Baugh and Cable (1993), Burrow and Turville-Petre (1992/2005); Culpeper 2005; Mitchell and Robinson (1992); and Pyles and Algeo (1993).

[4] For further discussion of feudalistic societies represented in modern fantasy, see Thompson 1982 and Zanger 1982.

[5] My account of English and Old English sounds here is informed by Aitchison (1991) and Mitchell and Robinson (1992).

[6] Future work might well identify such speech acts as archaisms. For this investigation, however, it was not possible to substantiate them as archaic with reference to the existing research.

Chapter 4

[1] My analysis here is informed by Wright and Hope's (1996) account of time and tense in fiction, and by Stockwell's (2000: 25, 34–6).

2 The use of 'it' also adds to this effect, of course, but cannot be discussed in this chapter as it is technically deviant.

Chapter 5

1 A few, mostly writer/critics, have pointed to well-drawn characters in alternative world texts. De Camp (1976: 162) was impressed by Robert E. Howard's creation Conan, Le Guin (1975/1993: 10) found much to praise in Nobusuke Tagomi in Philip K. Dick's *The Man in the High Castle*, Carter (1973: 100) was impressed by the characterization in Peake's *Titus Groan*, and Hunt (in Hunt and Lenz 2001/2004: 9) found in Pratchett's Discworld novels characters that were 'psychologically recognizable'.

2 Moylan (1986) has also discussed character, but his approach is so narrow that it is difficult to apply elsewhere. For him, characters are well-drawn and worthy if they resist capitalism, poorly drawn and unworthy if they do not.

3 This analysis is based on Halliday's (1973) work on transitivity, which, as Toolan (1988: 112) notes, can be very effectively applied in the study of literary character.

4 Extracts were transcribed from the collection of Borg-related *Star Trek* episodes compiled and released on DVD as *The Borg Fan Collective*.

5 Occasionally, individual Borg are selected to speak in certain story lines. The example of Hugh, discussed later on this chapter, is an example. Other examples include the Borg Queen, 7 of 9, and Locutus.

6 For the technical definition of a positive response (as opposed to a negative one, a challenge or a temporization), see Tsui (1994).

Bibliography

Primary Sources

Aldiss, B. 1978. 'Three Ways' in *New Arrivals, Old Encounters*. 1983. London: Triad Panther. 27–55.

—1973. 'A Spot of Konfrontation' in *New Arrivals, Old Encounters*. 1983. London: Triad Panther. 78–96.

—1966. 'Amen and Out' in *New Arrivals, Old Encounters*. 1983. London: Triad Panther. 56–77.

Baxter, S. 2007. *Conqueror. Time's Tapestry Book Two*. London: Gollancz.

Berman, R. and Braga, B. 2003. *Star Trek: Enterprise*. 'Regeneration', *Star Trek Borg Fan Collective* DVD. 2006.CBS/Paramount Pictures.

Berman, R., Piller, M. and Taylor, J. 1992. *Star Trek: Voyager*. 'Scorpion, Part 1', *Star Trek Borg Fan Collective* DVD. 2006. CBS/Paramount Pictures.

Burgess, A. 1962/1996. *A Clockwork Orange*. London: Penguin Books.

Dart-Thornton, C. 2002/2003. *The Lady of the Sorrows*. The Bitterbynde Trilogy Book Two. London: Tor/Pan Macmillan.

Donaldson, S. 1977/1978. *Lord Foul's Bane. The First Chronicles of Thomas Covenant, The Unbeliever*. Glasgow: Fontana Collin.

Dunsany, Lord. 1924/1969. *The King of Elfland's Daughter*. New York: Ballantine Books.

Hobb, R. 2005-7. The Soldier Son Trilogy (*Shaman's Crossing, Forest Mage, Renegade's Magic*). London: Harper Voyager.

—1999. *The Mad Ship*. The Liveship Traders Book Two. London: HarperCollins.

—1996. *Assassin's Apprentice*. The Farseer Trilogy Book One. London: HarperCollins.

Howard, R. 1973. *Conan the Adventurer*. Ed. by L. Sprague de Camp. London: Sphere Books Ltd. Stories analysed from this collection: 'The People of the Black Circle' 1934; 'The Slithering Shadow'1933; 'The Pool of the Black One' 1933.

Martin, G. R. R. 1996. *A Game of Thrones*. Book One of A Song of Ice and Fire. London: Voyager.

Moorcock, M. 2001. *Elric*. Fantasy Masterworks edition. London: Gollancz. This edition includes *The Dreaming City*, 1961; *While the Gods Laugh*, 1962; *The Stealer of Souls*, 1962; *Kings in Darkness*, 1962; *The Caravan of Forgotten Dreams*, 1962; *Stormbringer*, 1965, 1977.

Rodenberry, G. 1992. Star Trek: The Next Generation. 'I, Borg' *Star Trek Borg Fan Collective* DVD. 2006. CBS/Paramount Pictures.

—1990. *Star Trek: The Next Generation.* 'The Best of Both Worlds, Part 1', *Star Trek Borg Fan Collective* DVD. 2006. CBS/Paramount Pictures.

—1990. *Star Trek: The Next Generation.* 'The Best of Both Worlds, Part 2', *Star Trek Borg Fan Collective* DVD. 2006. CBS/Paramount Pictures.

—1989. Star Trek: The Next Generation. 'Q Who?', *Star Trek Borg Fan Collective* DVD. 2006. CBS/Paramount Pictures.

The Beautiful Journey. 2009. Wildworks in association with Theatre Royal Plymouth and culture,[10] supported by Find Your Talent and The Customs House. 28 July–8 August.

Whedon, J. 2002. *Firefly: The Complete Series* DVD. Mutant Enemy, Inc. in association with Twentieth Century Fox Home Entertainment, 2004.

Williams, T. 1996–2001. *Otherland.* Volumes 1–4. (*City of Golden Shadow*, 1996/1998; *River of Blue Fire*, 1998/1999; *Mountain of Black Glass*, 1999/2000; *Sea of Silver Light*, 2001/2002). London: Orbit.

Wyndham, J. 1968/1970. *Chocky.* Harmondsworth, Middlesex: Penguin Books.

References

Adamson, S. 1989. 'With Double Tongue: Diglossia, Stylistics, and the Teaching of English' in Short, M. (ed.). 1989. *Reading, Analysing and Teaching Literature.* 204–40. London and New York: Longman.

Aitchison, J. 1991. *Language Change: Progress or Decay?* 2nd edn. Cambridge: Cambridge University Press.

Aldiss, B. 2001. 'Introduction' in Aldiss, B. and Wingrove, D. 2001/1986. *Trillion Year Spree.* i–xii. North Yorkshire: House of Stratus.

Aldiss, B. and Wingrove, D. 1986/2001. *Trillion Year Spree.* North Yorkshire: House of Stratus. First published by Aldiss as *Billion Year Spree* in 1973.

Alessio, D. 2001 ' "Things are Different Now"?: A Post-Colonial Analysis of *Buffy the Vampire Slayer*', *European Legacy* 6.6: 731–40.

Amis, K. 1960/1963. *New Maps of Hell.* London: Four Square Books.

Anderson, A. S. 1988. 'Lord Dunsany: The Potency of Words and the Wonder of Things', *Mythlore* 55: 10–12.

Aranga, C. 2007. 'Book Review: *Conqueror* by Stephen Baxter', *SciFi Dimensions.* URL (accessed April 2008): http://www.scifidimensions.com/Apr07).

Armitt, L. 2005. *Fantasy Fiction.* New York and London: Continuum.

—1996. *Theorising the Fantastic.* London: Arnold.

Armstrong, K. 2005. *A Short History of Myth.* Edinburgh and New York: Canongate.

Ashcroft, B., Griffiths, G. And Tiffin, H. 1989/2002. *The Empire Writes Back.* 2nd edn. New York: Routledge.

Ashley, M. 2005. *Transformations: The Story of the Science Fiction Magazines from 1950–1970.* The History of the Science Fiction Magazine Volume 2. Liverpool: Liverpool University Press.

Atherton, M. 2006. *Teach Yourself Old English.* London: Hodder Education.

Attebery, B. 2003. 'The Magazine Era' in James, E. and Mendleson, F. (eds). 2003. *The Cambridge Companion to Science Fiction*. 32–47. Cambridge: Cambridge University Press.

—1992. *Strategies of Fantasy*. Bloomington, IN: Indiana University Press.

Auerbach, N. 1997. *Our Vampires, Ourselves*. Chicago: University of Chicago Press.

Baldick, C. 1990. *The Concise Oxford Dictionary of Literary Terms*. Oxford and New York: Oxford University Press.

Baxter, S. 2007. *Conqueror: Time's Tapestry Book 2*. London: Gollancz.

Baugh, A. and Cable, T. 1993. *A History of the English Language*. 4th edn. London: Routledge.

Bernstein, B. 1966. 'Elaborated and Restricted Codes: Their Social Origins and Some Consequences' in Gumperz, J. and Hymes, D. (eds). 1966. *The Ethnography of Communication*. American Anthropologist 66 (6:2).

Bleiler, E.F. (ed.). 1982. *Science Fiction Writers: Critical Studies of the Major Authors from the Early Nineteenth Century to the Present Day*. 251–8. New York: Scribner.

Broderick, D. 2003. 'New Wave and Backwash: 1960–1980' in James, E. and Mendleson, F. (eds). 2003. *The Cambridge Companion to Science Fiction*. 48–63. Cambridge: Cambridge University Press.

Brooke-Rose, C. 1981. *A Rhetoric of the Unreal: Studies in Narrative and Structure, Especially of the Fantastic*. Cambridge: Cambridge University Press.

Brown, E. 2007. '*Conqueror* by Stephen Baxter', *The Guardian* 3 February.

Brown, P. and Levinson, S. 1978/1987. *Politeness: Some Universals in Language Usage*. Cambridge: Cambridge University Press.

Burrow, J.A. and Turville-Petre, t. 1992/2005. *A Book of Middle English*. 3rd edn. Oxford: Blackwell Publishing.

Cantrell, B. 1980. 'British Fairy Tradition in *The King of Elfland's Daughter*', *Romantist* 4–5: 51–3.

Carpenter, J. (ed.). 1981. *The Letters of J.R.R. Tolkien*. London: HarperCollins Publishers.

Carter, L. 1973. *Imaginary Worlds: The Art of Fantasy*. New York: Ballantine Books.

—1965/1979. *The Wizard of Lemuria*. London: W.H. Allen and Co. Ltd.

Carter R. and Simpson, P. (eds). 1989. *Language, Discourse and Literature*. London: Unwin Hyman.

Chadbourne, M. 2008. 'Adventures in the Darkest Depths of Our Minds', *The Telegraph* 12 April.

Chance, J. and Sievers, A. (eds). 2005. *Tolkien's Modern Middle Ages*. Houndmills, Basingstoke, Hampshire: Palgrave Macmillan.

Chandler, J. and McClane, M. (eds). 2008. *The Cambridge Companion to British Romantic Poetry*. Cambridge: Cambridge University Press.

Chatman, S. 1978. *Story and Discourse: Narrative Structure in Fiction and Film*. Ithaca, NY and London: Cornell University Press.

Chen, Janey. 1970. *A Practical English-Chinese Pronouncing Dictionary*. Rutland, VT and Tokyo, Japan: Charles E. Tuttle Company.

Cheyne, R. 2006. 'Ursula Le Guin and Translation', *Extrapolation* 47(3): 457–72.

Clareson, T. 1971. 'Introduction: The Critical Reception of Science Fiction' in Clareson, T. (ed.). 1971. *The Other Side of Realism.* ix–iv. Bowling Green: Bowling Green University Popular Press.

Clareson, T. (ed.). 1971. *The Other Side of Realism.* Bowling Green: Bowling Green University Popular Press.

Clarke, I. F. 1979. *The Pattern of Expectation 1644–2001.* London: Jonathan Cape.

Clute, J. 2003. 'Science Fiction from 1980 to the Present' in James, E. and Mendleson, F. (eds). 2003. *The Cambridge Companion to Science Fiction.* 64–77. Cambridge: Cambridge University Press.

Collings, M. R. 1986. 'Samuel R. Delany and John Wilkins: Artificial Languages, Science, and Science Fiction' in Collings, M. R. (eds). 1986. *Reflections on the Fantastic: Selected Essays from the Fourth International Conference on the Fantastic in the Arts.* 61–7. New York: Greenwood Press.

Conley, T. and Cain, S. (eds). 2006. *Encyclopedia of Fictional and Fantastic Languages.* Westport, CT: Greenwood Press.

Conn, M. 2001. 'The Cyberspatial Landscapes of William Gibson and Tad Williams', AUMLA: *Journal of the Australasian Universities Language and Literature Association* November 96: 207–19.

Connors, S. 2001. 'Lovecraft's "The Picture in the House"', *Explicator* 59 (3): 140–2.

Conrad, S. and Biber, D. (eds). 2001. *Variation in English Multi-Dimensional Studies.* Harlow, Essex: Longman/Pearson Education

Consalvo, M. 2004. 'Borg Babes, Drones, and the Collective: Reading Gender and the Body in *Star Trek*'. *Women's Studies in Communication* 27 (2): 177–203.

Cramer, K. 2003. 'Hard Science Fiction' in James, E. and Mendleson, F. (eds). 2003. *The Cambridge Companion to Science Fiction.* 186–96. Cambridge: Cambridge University Press.

Crystal, D. 2004/2005. *The Stories of English.* London: Penguin Books. First published by Allen Lane.

—1991. *A Dictionary of Linguistics and Phonetics.* 3rd edn. Oxford: Blackwell.

—1990. *The English Language.* London: Penguin Books.

—1988. *Rediscover English Grammar.* Harlow, Essex: Longman.

—1964. 'A Liturgical Language in a Linguistic Perspective', *New Blackfriars* 1964: 48–156.

Csicsery-Ronay, I. Jr. 2003. 'Marxist Theory and Science Fiction' in James, E. and Mendleson, F. (eds). 2003. *The Cambridge Companion to Science Fiction.* 113–24. Cambridge: Cambridge University Press.

—2002. 'Dis-Imagined Communities: Science Fiction and the Future of Nations' in Hollinger, V. and Gordon, J. (eds). 2002. *Edging into the Future: Science Fiction and Contemporary Cultural Transformation.* 217–37. Philadelphia: University of Pennsylvania Press.

Cuddon, J. A. 1998. *The Penguin Dictionary of Literary Terms and Literary Theory.* 4th edn revised by C. A. Preston. London: Penguin Books.

Culpeper, J. 2005. *History of English.* 2nd edn. London and New York: Routledge.

—2001. *Language and Characterisation: People in Plays and Other Texts*. Harlow, Essex: Pearson Education, Ltd.

Davidson, M. C. 1997. 'Did Shakespeare Consciously Use Archaic English?', *Early Modern Literary Studies*. Special Issue 1 (1997) 4: 14. URL (accessed 23 July 2009) http://purl.oclc.org/emls/si-01/si-01davidson.html

Dawson, D. 2005. 'English, Welsh and Elvish: Language, Loss, and Cultural Recovery in J.R.R. Tolkien's *The Lord of the Rings*' in Chance, J. and Sievers, A. (eds). 2005. *Tolkien's Modern Middle Ages*. 105–20. Houndmills, Basingstoke, Hampshire: Palgrave Macmillan.

De Bolt, J. (ed.). 1979. *Ursula K. Le Guin: Voyager to Inner Lands and to Outer Space*. Port Washington, NY and London: National University Publications/ Kennikat Press.

de Camp, L. Sprague. 1976. *Literary Swordsmen and Sorcerers*. Sauk City, WI: Arkham House.

Delany, S. 1977. *The Jewel-Hinged Jaw: Notes on the Language of Science Fiction*. Elizabeth Town, NY: Dragon Press.

—1969. 'About Five Thousand One Hundred and Seventy-five Words', *Extrapolation* 10(2): 52–66.

Del Rey, L. 1979. *The World of Science Fiction: The History of a Subculture*. New York: Del Rey.

Disch, T. 2007. *Thomas Disch's Science Fiction Picks*. URL. http://www.writersreps.com.

Drabble, M. (ed.). 2000. *The Oxford Companion to English Literature*. 6th edn. Oxford: Oxford University Press.

Duncan, A. 2003. 'Alternate History' in James, E. and Mendleson, F. (eds). 2003. *The Cambridge Companion to Science Fiction*. 209–18. Cambridge: Cambridge University Press.

Eagleton, T. 1983. *Literary Theory: An Introduction*. Oxford: Blackwell.

Eckhardt, J.C. 1991. 'The Cosmic Yankee' in Schultz, D. and Joshi, S. (eds). 1991. *An Epicure in the Terrible: A Centennial Anthology of Essays in Honor of H.P. Lovecraft*. Cranbury, NJ: Associated University Presses.

Elfenein, A. 2008. 'Romantic Poetry and the Standardisation of English' in Chandler, J. and McClane, M. (eds). 2008. *The Cambridge Companion to British Romantic Poetry*. 76–97. Cambridge: Cambridge University Press.

Erard, M. 2008. 'English as She Will Be Spoke', *New Scientist* 29 March: 28–32.

Espenson, J. (ed.). 2004. *Finding Serenity: Anti-heroes, Lost Shepherds and Space Hookers in Joss Whedon's* Firefly. Dallas: Benbella.

Fairclough, N. 1995. *Critical Discourse Analysis: The Critical Study of Language*. Harlow, Essex: Longman.

Fallís, G. 1976. 'Code-switching in Bilingual Chicano Poetry', *Hispania* 59(4): 877–86.

Firefly: The Official Companion Volume One. 2006. London: Titan.

Fitzmaurice, S. and Taavitsainen, I. (eds). 2007. *Methods in Historical Pragmatics*. Topics in Historical Linguistics 52, edited by Elizabeth Closs Traugott and Bernard Kortman. Berlin and New York: Mouton de Gruyter.

Forster, E.M. 1927/2000. *Aspects of the Novel*. London: Penguin Classics. First published by Edward Arnold.

Fowler, R. (ed.). 1987. *A Dictionary of Modern Critical Terms.* Revised and enlarged edn. London and New York: Routledge and Kegan Paul.

Fredericks, S. C. 1978. 'Problems of Fantasy', *Science Fiction Studies* 14 (5:1): 1–12.

Friend, B. 1973. 'Strange Bedfellows: Science Fiction, Linguistics, and Education', *English Journal* 62: 998–1003.

Frye, N. 1957. *Anatomy of Criticism: Four Essays.* Princeton and Oxford: Princeton University Press.

Gardner-Chloros, P. et al. 2000. 'Parallel Patterns? A Comparison of Monolingual Speech and Bilingual Codeswitching Discourse', *Journal of Pragmatics* 32: 1305–41.

Goffman, I. 1967. *Interaction Ritual: Essays on Face to Face Behaviour.* Garden City, New York: Anchor Books.

Greenbaum, S. and Quirk, R. 1990. *A Student's Grammar of the English Language.* Harlow, Essex: Longman.

Griffin, B. and Wingrove, D. 1984. *Apertures: A Study of the Writings of Brian W. Aldiss.* Westport, CT: Greenwood Press.

Gross, S. 2000. 'Intentionality and the Markedness Model in Literary Codeswitching', *Journal of Pragmatics* 32: 1283–1303.

Gumperz, J. 1982. *Discourse Strategies.* Cambridge: Cambridge University Press.

Halliday, M.A.K. 1973. 'Linguistic Function and Literary Style: An Inquiry into the Language of William Golding's *The Inheritors*' in Weber, J.J. (ed.). 1996. *The Stylistics Reader: From Roman Jakobson to the Present.* 56–86. London: Arnold.

Hardy, S. 2003. 'A Story of Days to Come: H.G. Wells and the Language of Science Fiction', *Language and Literature* 12(3): 199–212.

Havens, C. 2003. *Joss Whedon: The Genius Behind Buffy.* Dallas, TX: Benbella.

Hedrick, T. 1996. 'Spik in Glyph? Translation, Wordplay, and Resistance in Chicano Bilingual Poetry', *The Translator* 2(2): 141–60.

Henighan, T. 1999. *Brian W. Aldiss.* New York: Twayne Publishers.

'Here's How it Was: The Making of *Firefly*'. *Firefly: The Complete Series.* Creator Joss Whedon, 2002. DVD Mutant Enemy/20th Century Fox, 2003.

Herman, V. 1995. *Dramatic Discourse.* London: Routledge.

Hillegas, M. 1979. 'The Literary Background to Science Fiction' in Parrinder, P. (ed.). 1979. *Science Fiction: A Critical Guide.* 1–17. London and New York: Longman.

—1971. 'Science Fiction as a Cultural Phenomenon: A Re-Evaluation' in Clareson, T. (ed.). 1971. *The Other Side of Realism.* 272–81. Bowling Green: Bowling Green University Popular Press.

Hinnenkamp, V. 2003. 'Mixed Language Varieties of Migrant Adolescents and the Discourse of Hybridity', *Journal of Multilingual and Multicultural Development* 24 (1,2): 12–41.

—1984. 'Eye-Witnessing Pidginization? Structural and Sociolinguistic Aspects of German and Turkish Foreigner Talk', *York Papers in Linguistics*, Volume 2: 153–66. Papers from the York Creole Conference, 24–27 September.

Hoey, M. 2007. 'Lexical Priming and Literary Creativity' in Hoey, M., et al. (eds). *Text, Discourse, and Corpora: Theory and Analysis.* 7–30. London: Continuum.

—2000. 'Disguising Doom: A Study of the Linguistic Features of Audience Manipulation in Michael Moorcock's *The Eternal Champion*', in Seed, D. (ed.). 2000. *Imagining Apocalypse: Studies in Cultural Crisis.* 151–65. Houndmills, Basingstoke, Hampshire: Macmillan.

Hoey, M., Mahlberg, M., Stubbs, M., and Wolfgang, T. (eds). 2007. *Text, Discourse, and Corpora: Theory and Analysis.* London: Continuum.

Hollinger, V. 2002. 'Apocalypse Comma' in Hollinger, V. and Gordon, J. (eds). 2002. *Edging into the Future: Science Fiction and Contemporary Cultural Transformation.* 159–73. Philadelphia: University of Pennsylvania Press.

—2000. 'A Language of the Future': Discourse Constructions for the Subject in *A Clockwork Orange* and Random Acts of Senseless Violence' in Sawyer, A. and Seed, D. (eds). 2000. *Speaking Science Fiction: Dialogue and Interpretations.* 82–95. Liverpool: Liverpool University Press.

—1991. 'Cybernetic Deconstructions: Cyberpunk and Postmodernism' in McCaffery, L. (ed.). 1991. *Storming the Reality Studio: A Casebook of Cyberpunk and Postmodernism.* 203–18. Durham, NC and London: Duke University Press.

Hollinger, V. and Gordon, J. 2002. 'Introduction' in Hollinger, V. and Gordon, J. (eds). 2002. *Edging into the Future: Science Fiction and Contemporary Cultural Transformation.* 1–8. Philadelphia: University of Pennsylvania Press.

Hollinger, V. and Gordon, J. (eds). 2002. *Edging into the Future: Science Fiction and Contemporary Cultural Transformation.* Philadelphia: University of Pennsylvania Press.

Horskotte, M. 2004. *The Postmodern Fantastic in Contemporary British Fiction.* Trier: Wissenschaftlicher Verlag Trier.

Hume, K. 1984. *Fantasy and Mimesis: Responses to Reality in Western Literature.* London: Methuen.

Hunt, P. and Lenz, M. 2001/2004. *Alternative Worlds in Fantasy Fiction.* New York and London: Continuum.

Hunt, P. and Ray, S. (eds). *International Companion Encyclopedia of Children's Literature.* London and New York: Routledge.

Inayatullah, N. 2003. 'Bumpy Space: Imperialisation and Resistance in Star Trek: The Next Generation' in Weldes, J. (ed.). 2003. *To Seek Out New Worlds.* 53–75. New York: Palgrave Macmillan.

Irwin, B. 1987. 'Archaic Pronouns in *The Lord of the Rings*', *Mythlore* 14 (1[51]): 46–7.

Irwin, W. R. 1976. *The Game of the Impossible: A Rhetoric of Fantasy.* Urbana, IL: University of Illinois Press.

Isaacs, N. D. and Zimbardo, R. A. (eds). 1968. *Tolkien and the Critics.* 164–9. Notre Dame, IN: University of Notre Dame Press.

Jackson, R. 1981. *Fantasy: The Literature of Subversion.* London and New York: Methuen.

Jackson, P. T. and Nexon, D. H. 2003. 'Representation is Futile? American Anti-Collectivisim and the Borg' in Weldes, J. (ed.). 2003. *To Seek out New Worlds: Science Fiction and World Politics.* 143–168. New York: Palgrave Macmillan.

Jacobs, A. and Jucker, A. 1995. 'The Historical Perspective in Pragmatics' in Jacobs, A. and Jucker, A. (eds). 1995. *Historical Pragmatics: Pragmatic*

Developments in the History of English. Pragmatics and Beyond New Series 35. 3–33. Amsterdam and Philadelphia: John Benjamins.

Jacobs, A. and Jucker, A. (eds) 1995. *Historical Pragmatics: Pragmatic Developments in the History of English.* Pragmatics and Beyond New Series 35. Amsterdam and Philadelphia: John Benjamins.

James, E. 2003. 'Utopias and Anti-Utopias' in James, E. and Mendleson, F. (eds). 2003. *The Cambridge Companion to Science Fiction.* 219–29. Cambridge: Cambridge University Press.

James, E. and Mendlesohn, F. 2003. 'Introduction' in James, E. and Mendleson, F. (eds). 2003. *The Cambridge Companion to Science Fiction.* 1–12. Cambridge: Cambridge University Press.

James, E. and Mendlesohn, F. (eds). 2003. *The Cambridge Companion to Science Fiction.* Cambridge: Cambridge University Press.

Kastovsky, D. and Mettinger, A. (eds). 2000. *The History of English in a Social Context.* Trends in Linguistic Studies and Monographs 129, ed. by Werner Winter. Berlin and New York: Mouton de Gruyter.

Kavanagh, D., Keohane, K., and Kuhling, C. 2001. 'Reading *Star Trek*: Imagining, Theorizing, and Reflecting on Organizational Discourse and Practice', in Simth, M. Higgins, M., Parker, M. and Lightfoot, G. (eds.). 2001. *Science Fiction and Organization.* 125–42. London: RoutledgeJackson and Nexon 2003.

Ketterer, D. 1974. *New Worlds for Old: The Apocalyptic Imagination, Science Fiction, and American Literature.* Bloomington, IN: Indiana University Press.

Kohnen, T. 2004. ' "Let Mee Bee So Bold to Request You to Tell Mee": Constructions with Let Me and the History of English Directives', *Journal of Historical Pragmatics* 5(1): 159–73.

Kreml, N. 1998. 'Implications of Styleswitching in the Narrative Voice of Cormac McCarthy's *All the Pretty Horses*' in Myers-Scotton, C. (ed.). *Codes and Consequences.* 141–61. New York: Oxford University Press.

Labov, W. 1972. *Language in the Inner City: Studies in the Black English Vernacular.* Philadelphia: University of Pennsylvania Press.

Latham, R. 2002. 'Mutant Youth: Posthuman Fantasies and High-Tech Consumption in 1990s Science Fiction' in Hollinger, V. and Gordon, J. (eds). 2002. *Edging into the Future: Science Fiction and Contemporary Cultural Transformation.* 124–41. Philadelphia: University of Pennsylvania Press.

Lauterbach, E. and Clareson, T. 1959. 'From the Launching Pad', *Extrapolation* 1 (1): 1.

Leech, G. 1969. *A Linguistic Guide to English Poetry.* London: Longman.

Leech, G. and Short, M. 1981/2007. *Style in Fiction.* Edinburgh: Pearson Education.

Lefanu, S. 1988. *In the Chinks of the World Machine: Feminism and Science Fiction.* London: The Women's Press.

Le Guin, U. 1993. *The Language of the Night: Essays on Fantasy and Science Fiction.* New revised edn. New York: Harper Perennial. First published in 1979 by G. P. Putnam's Sons.

—1989/1993. 'Preface to the 1989 edition' in *The Language of the Night: Essays on Fantasy and Science Fiction.* 1–5. New revised edn. New York: Harper Perennial. First published in 1979 by G. P. Putnam's Sons.

—1979/1993. 'Introduction', in *The Language of the Night: Essays on Fantasy and Science Fiction.* 29–33. New revised edn. New York: Harper Perennial. First published in 1979 by G. P. Putnam's Sons.

—1977/1993. 'Introduction to Rocannon's World' in *The Language of the Night: Essays on Fantasy and Science Fiction.* 129–33. New revised edn. New York: Harper Perennial. First published in 1979 by G. P. Putnam's Sons.

—1976/1993. 'Is Gender Necessary? Redux', in *The Language of the Night: Essays on Fantasy and Science Fiction.* 155–172. New revised edn. New York: Harper Perennial. First published in 1979 by G. P. Putnam's Sons.

—1974/1993. 'Why are Americans Afraid of Dragons', in *The Language of the Night: Essays on Fantasy and Science Fiction.* 34–40. New revised edn. New York: Harper Perennial. First published in 1979 by G. P. Putnam's Sons.

—1973/1993. 'From Elfland to Poughkeepsie' in *The Language of the Night: Essays on Fantasy and Science Fiction.* 78–92. New revised edn. New York: Harper Perennial. First published in 1979 by G. P. Putnam's Sons.

Lehiste, I. 1988. *Lectures on Language Contact.* Cambridge, MA and London, England: The MIT Press.

Lenker, U. 2007. '*Soplice, Forsoothe, Truly* – Communicative Principles and Invited Inferences in the History of Truth-Intensifying Adverbs in English' in Fitzmaurice, S. and Taavitsainen, I. (eds). 2007. *Methods in Historical Pragmatics.* Topics in Historical Linguistics 52, edited by Elizabeth Closs Traugott and Bernard Kortman. 81–105. Berlin and New York: Mouton de Gruyter.

LePage, R. B. and Tabouret-Keller, A. 1985. *Acts of Identity: Creole-based Approaches to Language and Ethnicity.* London: Cambridge University Press.

Levinson, S. 1983. *Pragmatics.* Cambridge: Cambridge University Press.

Levorato, A. 2003. *Language and Gender in the Fairy Tale Tradition: A Linguistic Analysis of Old and New Storytelling.* Houndmills, Basingstoke, Hampshire: Palgrave Macmillan.

Lewis, C.S. 1961. *An Experiment in Criticism.* Cambridge: Cambridge University Press.

Lister, M. 1988. *The European Community and the Developing World: The Role of the Lomé Convention.* Aldershot: Avebury.

Luckhurst, R. 2005. *Science Fiction.* Cambridge: Polity Press.

Lynch, A. 2005. 'Archaism, Nostalgia, and Tennysonian War in *The Lord of the Rings*' in Chance, J. and Sievers, A. (eds). 2005. *Tolkien's Modern Middle Ages.* 77–92. Houndmills, Basingstoke, Hampshire: Palgrave Macmillan.

Macleod, K. 2003. 'Politics and Science Fiction' in James, E. and Mendlesohn, F. (eds). 2003. *The Cambridge Companion to Science Fiction.* 230–40. Cambridge: Cambridge University Press.

Mandala, S. 2008. 'Representing the Future: Chinese and Codeswitching in Firefly' in Wilcox, R. and Cochran, T. (eds). *Investigating Firefly and Serenity: Science Fiction on the Frontier.* 31–40. London and New York: I.B. Tauris.

Manlove, C. 1999. *The Fantasy Literature of England.* Hampshire: Palgrave.

—1982. 'On the Nature of Fantasy' in Schlobin, R. (ed.). 1982. *The Aesthetics of Fantasy Literature and Art.* Indiana, USA and Sussex, UK: University of Notre Dame Press and The Harvester Press.

—1975. *Modern Fantasy: Five Studies*. Cambridge: Cambridge University Press.

Mathews, R. 1977. *Aldiss Unbound: The Science Fiction of Brian W. Aldiss*. San Bernadine, CA: The Borgo Press.

Mazzon, G. 2009. *Interactive Dialogue Sequences in Middle English Drama*. Amsterdam/Philadelphia: John Benjamins.

—2000. 'Social Relations and Forms of Address in The Canterbury Tales' in Kastovsky, D. and Mettinger, A. (eds). 2000. *The History of English in a Social Context*. Trends in Linguistic Studies and Monographs 129. 135–68. Berlin and New York: Mouton de Gruyter.

McCaffery, L. 1991. 'Introduction' in McCaffery, L. (ed.). 1991. *Storming the Reality Studio: A Casebook of Cyberpunk and Postmodern Science Fiction*. 1–16. Durham, NC and London: Duke University Press.

McCaffery, L. (ed.). 1991. *Storming the Reality Studio: A Casebook of Cyberpunk and Postmodern Science Fiction*. 1–16. Durham, NC and London: Duke University Press.

McHale, B. 1991. 'POSTcyberMODERNpunkISM' in McCaffery, L. (ed.). 1991. *Storming the Reality Studio: A Casebook of Cyberpunk and Postmodern Science Fiction*. 308–23. Durham, NC and London: Duke University Press.

McNelly, W. E. 1982. 'Brian W. Aldiss 1925–' in Bleiler, E. F. (ed.). 1982. *Science Fiction Writers: Critical Studies of the Major Authors from the Early Nineteenth Century to the Present Day*. 251–8. New York: Scribner.

Mendieta-Lombardo, E. and Cintron, Z. 1995. 'Marked and Unmarked Choices of Code Switching in Bilingual Poetry', *Hispania* 78 (3): 565–72.

Mendlesohn, F. 2003. 'Religion and Science Fiction' in James, E. and Mendlesohn, F. (eds). 2003. *The Cambridge Companion to Science Fiction*. 264–75. Cambridge: Cambridge University Press.

Meyers, W. 1980. *Aliens and Linguists: Language Study and Science Fiction*. Athens, GA: University of Georgia Press.

Minugh, D. 1999. 'What Aileth Thee, to Print so Curiously? Archaic Forms and Contemporary Newspaper Language' in Taavitsainen, I. et al. (eds). 1999. *Writing in Nonstandard English*. 285–304. Pragmatics and Beyond New Series 67. Amsterdam and Philadelphia: John Benjamins.

Mitchell, B. and Robinson, C. 1992. *A Guide to Old English*. Oxford: Blackwell.

Mobley, J. 1973. 'Toward a Definition of Fantasy Fiction', *Extrapolation* 15: 117–28.

Moody, N. 2000. 'Aphasia and Mother Tongue: Themes of Language Creation and Silence in Women's Science Fiction' in Sawyer, A. and Seed, D. (eds). 2000. *Speaking Science Fiction: Dialogues and Interpretations*. 179–87. Liverpool: Liverpool University Press.

Moylan, T. 1986. *Demand the Impossible: Science Fiction and the Utopian Imagination*. London and New York: Methuen.

Myers, V. 1983. 'Conversational Technique in Ursula LeGuin: A Speech-Act Analysis', *Science Fiction Studies*. 10: 306–16.

Myers-Scotton, C. 2000. 'Explaining the Role of Norms and Rationality in Codeswitching', *Journal of Pragmatics* 32: 1259–71.

—1993. *Social Motivations for Codeswitching*. Oxford: Clarendon.

Nevalainen, T. And Raumolin-Bronberg, H. 1995. 'Constraints on Politeness: The Pragmatics of Address Formulae in Early English Correspondence' in

Jacobs, A. and Jucker, A. (eds) 1995. *Historical Pragmatics: Pragmatic Developments in the History of English.* 541–601. Pragmatics and Beyond New Series 35. Amsterdam and Philadelphia: John Benjamins.

Nicholls, P. 1979. *The Encyclopedia of Science Fiction.* London: Granada.

Nurmi, A., Nevala, M. and Palander-Collin, M. (eds). 2009. *The Language of Daily Life in England 1400–1800.* Amsterdam and Philadelphia: John Benjamins.

Palander-Collin, M. 2009. 'Patterns of Interaction, Self-Mention, and Addressee Inclusion in the Letters of Nathaniel Bacon and His Correspondents' in Nurmi, A. et al. (eds). 2009. *The Language of Daily Life in England 1400–1800.* 53–74. Amsterdam and Philadelphia: John Benjamins.

Parker, D. 1956. 'Hwæt We Holbytla . . .', *Hudson Review* 9: 598–609.

Parrinder, P. (ed.). 2000. *Learning from Otherworlds: Estrangement, Cognition and the Politics of Science Fiction and Utopia.* Liverpool: Liverpool University Press.

Parrinder, P. 1979a. 'Editor's Introduction' in Parrinder, P. (ed.). 1979. *Science Fiction: A Critical Guide.* vii–x. London and New York: Longman.

Parrinder, P. 1979b. 'The Alien Encounter: Or, Ms Brown and Mrs LeGuin' in Parrinder, P. (ed.). 1979. *Science Fiction: A Critical Guide.* 148–61. London and New York: Longman. First appeared in 1976 in *Science Fiction Studies* 3(1).

Parrinder, P. (ed.). 1979. *Science Fiction: A Critical Guide.* London and New York: Longman.

Pfeiffer, J. 1979. '"But Dragons Have Keen Ears": On Hearing *Earthsea* with Recollections of Beowulf' in De Bolt, J. (ed.). 1979. *Ursula K. LeGuin: Voyager to Inner Lands and to Outer Space.* Port Washington, NY and London: National University Publications/Kennikat Press.

Pyles, T. and Algeo, J. 1993. *The Origins and Development of the English Language.* New York: Harcourt Brace.

Rabkin, E. 1976. *The Fantastic in Literature.* Princeton, NJ: Princeton University Press.

Rey, J. 2001. 'Changing Gender Roles in Popular Culture: Dialogue in *Star Trek* Episodes from 1966–1993' in Conrad, S. and Biber, D. (eds). 2001. *Variation in English Multi-Dimensional Studies.* Harlow, Essex: Longman/Pearson Education.

Reynolds, P. 1987. 'Looking Forwards from the Tower: The Relationship of the Dark Ages in Northern Europe to Fantasy Literature', *Mythlore* 52: 5–10.

Richardson, A. 1994. 'Archaism and Modernity: Poetic Diction, Period Style and the Romantic Canon', *Southern Humanities Review* 28(3): 209–28.

Roberts, A. 2006. *Science Fiction.* 2nd edn. London and New York: Routledge.

—2000. *Science Fiction.* London and New York Routledge.

Rose, M. 1981. *Alien Encounters: Anatomy of Science Fiction.* Cambridge, MA and London: Harvard University Press.

Russ, J. 1975. 'Towards an Aesthetic of Science Fiction', *Science Fiction Studies* 2(2): 112–19.

Ryder, M. 2003. 'I Met Myself Coming and Going: Co(?)-Referential Noun Phrases and Point of View in Time Travel Stories', *Language and Literature* 12 (3): 213–32.

Sanders, S. 1979. 'The Disappearance of Character' in Parrinder, P. (ed.). 1979. *Science Fiction: A Critical Guide.* 131–47. London and New York: Longman.

Sawyer, A. and Seed, D. (eds). 2000. *Speaking Science Fiction: Dialogues and Interpretations.* Liverpool: Liverpool University Press.

Schlobin, R. (ed.). 1982. *The Aesthetics of Fantasy Literature and Art.* Indiana, USA and Sussex, England: University of Notre Dame Press and The Harvester Press.

Schmerl, R. 1971. 'Fantasy as Technique' in Clareson, T. (ed.). 1971. *The Other Side of Realism.* 105–15. Bowling Green: Bowling Green University Popular Press.

Scholes, R. 1975. *Structural Fabulation.* Notre Dame and London: University of Notre Dame Press.

Schultz, D. and Joshi, S. (eds). 1991. *An Epicure in the Terrible: A Centennial Anthology of Essays in Honor of H.P. Lovecraft.* Cranbury, NJ: Associated University Presses.

Schweitzer, D. 1997. 'How Much of Dunsany is Worth Reading' in *Windows of the Imagination: Essays on Fantasy Literature.* 122–8. San Bernardino, CA: Borgo Press.

—1989. *Pathways to Elfland: The Writings of Lord Dunsany.* Philadelphia, PA: Owlswick Press.

Schwetman, J. 1985. 'Russell Hoban's *Riddley Walker* and the Language of the Future', *Extrapolation* 26(3): 212–19.

Searle, J. R. 1979. *Expression and Meaning: Studies in the Theory of Speech Acts.* Cambridge: Cambridge University Press.

—1969. *Speech Acts: An Essay in the Philosophy of Language.* Cambridge and New York: Cambridge University Press.

Sebba, M. 1997. *Contact Languages: Pidgins and Creoles.* London: Macmillan.

Seed, D. 2004. *The Fictions of Mind Control: A Study of Novels and Films Since World War II.* Kent, OH and London: the Kent State University Press.

—1999. American Science Fiction and the Cold War: Literature and Film. Edinburgh: Edinburgh University Press.

Seed, D. (ed.). 2004. *Imagining Apocalypse: Studies in Cultural Crisis.* Houndmills, Basingstoke, Hampshire: Macmillan.

—1995. *Anticipations: Essays on Early Science Fiction and Its Precursors.* Liverpool: Liverpool University Press.

Shaw, P. and Stockwell, P. (eds). 1991. *Subjectivity and Literature from the Romantics to the Present Day.* 101–12. London: Pinter Publishers.

Shippey, T. 1982. *The Road to Middle-Earth.* London: George Allen and Unwin.

—1977. 'The Magic Art and the Evolution of Words: Ursula LeGuin's *Earthsea Trilogy*', *Mosaic* XI(2): 147–63.

Short, M. 1989. 'Discourse Analysis and the Analysis of Drama', in Carter R. and Simpson, P. (eds). 1989. *Language, Discourse and Literature.* 139–68. London: Unwin Hyman.

Short, M. (ed.). 1989. *Reading, Analysing and Teaching Literature.* London and New York: Longman.

Short, S. 2004. 'The Federation and Borg Value-Systems in *Star Trek*'. *Foundation* 92: 31–50.

Sonmez, M. 2002. 'Archaisms in "The Rime of the Ancient Mariner"', *Cardiff Corvey: Reading the Romantic Text*. Issue 9. URL (accessed 22 July 2009) http://www.cf.ac.uk/encap/corvey/articles/cco9_n02.html

Stevens, C. 1984. *EEC and The Third World: A Survey 4: Renegotiating Lomé*. London: Hodder and Stoughton in Association with the Overseas Development Institute and the Institute of Development Studies.

Stockwell, P. 2003a. 'Introduction: Science Fiction and Literary Linguistics', *Language and Literature* 12(3): 195–8.

—2003b. 'Schema Poetics and Speculative Cosmology', *Language and Literature* 12(3): 252–71.

—2000. *The Poetics of Science Fiction*. Harlow, Essex: Longman.

Stockwell, P. 1991. 'Language, Knowledge, and the Stylistics of Science Fiction' in Shaw, P. and Stockwell, P. (eds). 1991. *Subjectivity and Literature from the Romantics to the Present Day*. 101–12. London: Pinter Publishers.

Sullivan, K. 2004. 'Chinese Words in the 'Verse' in Espenson, J. (ed.). *Finding Serenity: Anti-heroes, Lost Shepherds and Space Hookers in Joss Whedon's* Firefly. 197–207. Dallas: Benbella.

Sullivan, C. W. III. 1996. 'High Fantasy' in Hunt, P. and Ray, S. (eds). *International Companion Encyclopedia of Children's Literature*. 303–13. London and New York: Routledge.

Suvin, D. 1979. *Metamorphoses of Science Fiction: On the Poetics and History of a Literary Genre*. New Haven and London: Yale University Press.

Swinfen, A. 1984. *In Defence of Fantasy*. London: Routledge and Kegan Paul.

Taavitsainen, I. And Jucker, A. 2007. 'Speech Act Verbs and Speech Acts in the History of English' in Fitzmaurice, S. and Taavitsainen, I. (eds). 2007. *Methods in Historical Pragmatics*. 107–38. Topics in Historical Linguistics 52, edited by Elizabeth Closs Traugott and Bernard Kortman. Berlin and New York: Mouton de Gruyter.

Taavitsainen, I., Melchers, G. and Pahta, P. (eds). 1999. *Writing in Non-Standard English*. Pragmatics and Beyond New Series 67. Edited by Andreas Jucker. Amsterdam and Philadelphia: John Benjamins.

Tallis, R. 1988. *In Defence of Realism*. London: Edward Arnold.

Tannen, D. 1989. *Talking Voices: Repetition, Dialogue and Imagery in Conversational Discourse*. Cambridge: Cambridge University Press.

Taylor, J. 1990. 'From Pulpstyle to Innerspace: The Stylistics of American New-Wave SF', *Style* 24(4): 611–27.

Thomason, S. 2001. *Language Contact*. Edinburgh: Edinburgh University Press.

Thompson, R. 1982. 'Modern Fantasy and Medieval Romance: A Comparative Study' in Schlobin, R. (ed.). 1982. *The Aesthetics of Fantasy Literature and Art*. 211–25. Indiana, USA and Sussex, England: University of Notre Dame Press and The Harvester Press.

Thun, N. 1963. *Reduplicative Words in English. A Study of Formations of the Type Tick-Tick, Hurly-Burly, and Shilly-Shally*. Lund: Carl Bloms Boktryckeri A.-B.

Timmerman, J. 1983. *Otherworlds: The Fantasy Genre*. Bowling Green: Bowling Green University Popular Press.

Tinkler, J. 1968. 'Old English in Rohan' in Isaacs, N. D. and Zimbardo, R. A. (eds). 1968. *Tolkien and the Critics*. 164–9. Notre Dame, IN: University of Notre Dame Press.

Todd, L. 1974/1990. *Pidgins and Creoles*. New edn. London and New York: Routledge.

Todorov, T. 1973. *The Fantastic: A Structural Approach to a Literary Genre*. Trans. by Richard Howard. Cleveland, OH: Case Western Reserve University Press. Originally published in 1970.

Tolkien, J. R. R. 1947/1964. 'On Fairy Stories' in *Tree and Leaf*. 11–70. London: Allen and Unwin.

Toolan, M. 1988. *Narrative: A Critical Linguistic Introduction*. London and New York: Routledge.

Trask, R. 1999. *Key Concepts in Language and Linguistics*. London and New York: Routledge.

Traugott, E. C. 1981. 'The Voice of Varied Linguistic and Cultural Groups in Fiction: Some Criteria for the Use of Language Varieties in Writing' in Whiteman, M. (ed.). 1981. *Writing: The Nature, Development, and Teaching of Written Communication. Volume1*. 111–36. New Jersey: Erlbaum Associates.

Traugott, E. C. and Pratt, M. L. 1980. *Linguistics for Students of Literature*. Fort Worth: Harcourt College Publishers.

Tsui, A. B. M. 1994. *English Conversation*. Oxford: Oxford University Press.

Ugolnik, A. 1977. 'Wordhord Onleac: The Medieval Sources of J.R.R. Tolkien's Linguistic Aesthetic', *Mosaic* 10(2): 15–31.

Wardhaugh, R. 1992. *An Introduction to Sociolinguistics*. 2nd edn. Cambridge: Blackwell.

Walsh, C. 2003. 'From "Capping" to Intercision: Metaphors/Metonyms of Mind Control in the Young Adult Fiction of John Christopher and Philip Pullman', *Language and Literature* 12(3): 233–251.

Weber, J. J. (ed.). 1996. *The Stylistics Reader: From Roman Jakobson to the Present*. London: Arnold.

Wei, Li. 2005a. 'Starting from the Right Place: Introduction to the Special Issue on Conversational Code-Switching', *Journal of Pragmatics* 37: 275–79.

Wei, Li. 2005b. ' "How Can You Tell?" Towards a Common Sense Explanation of Conversational Code-Switching', *Journal of Pragmatics* 37: 375–89.

Weldes, J. (ed.). 2003. *To Seek Out New Worlds*. New York: Palgrave Macmillan.

Westfahl, G. 2003. 'Space Opera' in James, E. and Mendlesohn, F. (eds). 2003. *The Cambridge Companion to Science Fiction*. 197–208. Cambridge: Cambridge University Press.

White, D. 1999. *Dancing with Dragons: Ursula K. LeGuin and the Critics*. Columbia, SC: Camden House.

Whiteman, M. (ed.). 1981. *Writing: The Nature, Development, and Teaching of Written Communication. Volume 1*. Mahwah, NJ: Erlbaum Associates.

Williams, A. 2005. 'Fighting Words and Challenging Expectations: Language Alternation and Social Roles in a Family Dispute', *Journal of Pragmatics* 37: 317–28.

Wilson, S. 1984. 'The Doctrine of Organic Unity: E R Eddison and the Romance Tradition', *Extrapolation* 25(1): 12–19.

Wingrove, D. 1979. 'Thinking in Fuzzy Sets: The Recent SF of Brian W. Aldiss', *Pacific Quarterly Moana* 4(3) July: 288–94.

Wolfe, G. 2002. 'Evaporating Genre: Strategies of Dissolution in the Postmodern Fantastic' in Hollinger, V. and Gordon, J. (eds). 2002. *Edging into the Future: Science Fiction and Contemporary Cultural Transformation.* 11–29. Philadelphia: University of Pennsylvania Press.

—1986. *Critical Terms for Science Fiction and Fantasy: A Glossary and Guide to Scholarship.* New York: Greenwood Press.

—1982. 'The Encounter with Fantasy' in Schlobin, R. (ed.). 1982. *The Aesthetics of Fantasy Literature and Art.* 1–15. Indiana, USA and Sussex, England: University of Notre Dame Press and The Harvester Press.

Wolmark, J. 1994. *Aliens and Others: Science Fiction, Feminism, and Postmodernism.* New York and London: Harvester Wheatsheaf.

—1986. 'Feminism and Science Fiction', *Foundation* 37: 48–51.

Woolf, V. 1924/1950. 'Mr Bennett and Mrs Brown' in *The Captain's Death-Bed and Other Essays.* London: Hogarth.

Wright, Leigh Adams. 2004. 'Asian Objects in Space' in Espenson, J. (ed.). 2004. *Finding Serenity: Anti-heroes, Lost Shepherds and Space Hookers in Joss Whedon's Firefly.* 29–35. Dallas, TX: Benbella.

Wright, L. and Hope, J. 1996: *Stylistics: A Practical Coursebook.* London: Routledge.

Zanger, J. 1982. 'Heroic Fantasy and Social Reality: *Ex Nihilo Nihil Fit*' in Schlobin, R. (ed.). 1982. *The Aesthetics of Fantasy Literature and Art.* 226–36. Indiana, USA and Sussex, England: University of Notre Dame Press and The Harvester Press.

Index

Lightning Source UK Ltd.
Milton Keynes UK
UKOW04f0347200614

233722UK00001B/31/P